ON THE STRENGTH

ON THE STRENGTH

The story of the British Army wife

VERONICA BAMFIELD

CHARLES KNIGHT & COMPANY LIMITED
LONDON AND TONBRIDGE

Charles Knight & Company Limited
25 New Street Square, London EC4A 3JA
& Sovereign Way, Tonbridge, Kent TN9 1RW

Distributed in Canada by
The General Publishing Company Limited, Toronto

© *Veronica Bamfield 1974*

ISBN 0 85314–231–9

Printed in Great Britain

FOR TICH BAMFIELD,

THE ROYAL WELCH FUSILIERS,

AND

TO THE MEMORY OF MY GRANDFATHER

LIEUTENANT-COLONEL HENRY WOOD, CB

THE RIFLE BRIGADE

Contents

List of Illustrations

Preface

THIS BOOK HAS been lurking in the back of my mind for years and yet, at the moment of realisation, I find myself thoroughly nervous. The reason for this unexpected and unenviable state is the anticipation of that mutter, possibly rising to a roar, of indignation from those who know things I have not discovered about people and places of which I have never heard. "Nothing about So and So or Such and Such . . . ?" Seize the ball-point; rip the cover off the typewriter; dash off a letter to tell her she doesn't know what she's talking about. Well, gentle reader, this is where I forestall you because before writing a word I discussed this very matter with my publisher, pointing out that in the time and number of pages allowed me there were bound to be some areas, geographical and historical, which remained uncharted. His reply was that he did not expect a definitive work but a lively, readable book containing as much information as could be packed into 60,000 words. In this I hope I have succeeded, leaving it to others to make further and later discoveries should they so wish.

So here we are then. A tough lot. We have had to be. For more than three hundred years we have travelled the world with our men, often at a moment's notice. We loved and courted, married and bore children here, there and everywhere over the globe. Our ghosts must surely haunt married quarters up and down the British Isles, in Gibraltar, Malta, Bermuda, Germany and the Curragh. We kept house in bungalows in India, Malaya, Mauritius, Hong Kong, Shanghai and the West Indies, far from the corrugated iron houses of South Africa or the cold of North America and Canada. We were the most experienced home-makers in the world, and we took that world wherever we went. This made us gossipy, parochial and often tiresome. We didn't really bother to get to know the countries we lived in. For most of the time we didn't have enough to do or to think about so we became shallow and stupid. But our faults did not outweigh our virtues, the greatest of which was bravery. We

9

endured capture, wounding, imprisonment, kidnapping, shipwreck, rape and murder, and a surprising number of us lived to tell our stories. Wherever we went (with the exception of the regimental depot) we were strangers. There because our husbands were, never really belonging. If our man died or was killed—out! Quickly and on a very small pension. This was the pattern up to the Second World War after which were brought about different and better conditions that play no part in this story, the story of the colonels' ladies and the Judy O'Gradys my mother and my grandmother knew. No one in their senses would want the bad old days back again though those of us who remember may regret the family feeling which has disappeared with the amalgamation of regiments and the resulting loss of traditions and characteristics. It is the old guard I salute in affectionate admiration as I write of the extraordinary life we took so much for granted. From them I am descended. To them by marriage I belong.

Acknowledgements

AT THE VERY top of the list of the many who have contributed to the writing of this book must come Mrs. Olive D'Arcy Hart who researched in the Public Record Office and the British Museum, moving with ease and surety in the (to me at any rate) nightmare maze of index numbers, and who from time to time came up with unexpected and delectable titbits tucked away among official reports and papers. A distinguished writer on military subjects, the Marquess of Anglesey, gave help and support over details and reading matter. This was particularly kind as he had never heard of me before. Mr. Edmund Brudenell, who must be well accustomed to answering queries about the famous Earl of Cardigan, seemed just as interested in supplying domestic details about his lordship's beautiful horse.

Thanks are due to Mr. Reynell Grissell for allowing the use of the Burgoyne account of Lady Harriet Acland's exploits and his letter to Mrs. Reynell. Mr. N. E. Willis, Director of the Wigan Record Office, gave me permission to quote from the diary of Anna

Walker; and Miss M. C. Hill, archivist of the Shropshire Record Office, has also given help and support. Brigadier Douglas Pringle, OBE, supplied valuable material relating to the Duke of York's Military School. Mr. Donald Clark, Headmaster of Princess Helena College, and Lt. Col. A. J. E. Cruikshank, MC, Bursar of The Royal School for Officers' Daughters at Bath, were also most helpful.

Dr. R. J. Bingle of the India Office Library obtained permission for me to quote from the diary of Madeleine Jackson. This diary, like that of Charlotte Owen, has never been published or used in quotation before, and I am grateful to Major F. S. G. Shore, Madeleine's grandson, and to Mr. Robert Owen, great-grandson of Charlotte, for permission to do so. Another grandmother to be proud of was Delia Peppe, whose grandson, Lt. Col. W. T. H. Peppe, DSO, OBE, MC, lent me an account of her life shortly before his death. I have indeed been fortunate in that so much material is from entirely private sources. Mr. A. L. Binney owns the tragic Lindsay letters and gave me permission to reproduce the photographs of the girls who perished at Cawnpore. I am grateful to Miss Rosa Ward, OBE, for the story of how, when she was a baby, she narrowly missed death from a falling rock and then by drowning when she fell from the houseboat in Kashmir.

Mrs. Bruxner-Randall and Mrs. Burton, both wives of the Royal Welch Fusiliers, gave me their stories verbatim. Miss Mary Walker sent me the Adams' letters, and the great-nieces and nephew of Mrs. Webber-Harris—Mrs. Hubbard, Mrs. Gairdner and Lt. Col. Andrew Man, DSO—have kindly allowed me to publish their great-aunt's account of the remarkable experiences that earned her a replica of the VC. I am grateful to Miss R. W. Verner for sending me the amusing little piece about the wife who accompanied her husband on a small pony and nearly succeeded in going into action with him from the *Reminiscence* of her great-grandfather, Col. William Verner, 7th Hussars. Miss Frances Briggs supplied the sad story of the young wife who died in Malta having travelled that far with her husband who was en route for the Crimea. Miss Frederica Tyrell had a remarkable great-grandmother who, pregnant and with eight children to look after, accompanied her husband to South Africa in 1850. Lady Wakeman gave me her memory of President Kruger's funeral, and Mrs. Ethel Heath, who heard I was writing a book, came up with the charming story of the iron-stand. Mrs. M. Stephens and Mr. Charles Gamble sent me the account of their grandmother, "the last of the army washerwomen". Miss Elmira Wade gave me the incident of the harp at Lucknow. Mrs. R. H. L. Green told me about "Aunt Louise", and Col. Denis Russell Roberts has allowed me to quote from *Spotlight on Singapore*.

Col. J. L. Corbett-Winder, OBE, MC, gave me access to the letters of his grandfather, Captain Corbett, and Major Michael Grissell supplied the photograph of the child on the gun. I believe another unique photograph to be that of Emily Polehampton, supplied by Mrs. Maud Hamer; details about this mutiny heroine were given to me by Denis Salt, OBE, of Shrewsbury. I have been more than lucky in having G. Archer Parfitt, Member of the Society for Army Historical Research, and Maurice E. Jones, a well-known authority on military music, as neighbours. They have been bombarded with questions and have answered them all.

I should not have got far without my friends: Joan Tate, who had odds and ends of chapters pushed under her nose to see if they read as sense to someone who knew nothing of the subject, or Beryl Leatham Thomas who came up with the title, over which I had been unsuccessfully racking my brains. And I would have got nowhere at all without Sandra Bunn who typed the MS so beautifully that the publisher thanked me for what he said was a positive treat!

Recently a military historian writing to me about one of his books said, "It was fun to do, as you can imagine." This book has been fun to do also. I hope it will be fun to read.

1. Marriage

FOR AS LONG as there has been recorded history, soldiers have married and their wives have borne them children. Some wives were good, some bad; some were faithful, some not, though probably few set about their infidelity quite as blatantly as Bathsheba, the wife of Uriah the Hittite, who allowed her lover, King David, to order her husband to be sent to the "forefront of the hottest battle ... that he may be stricken and die" (II Samuel 11:15). Many a British girl became the bride of a soldier in the Roman army of occupation; and the manning of all garrisons, and every victory or defeat from the Crusades to Cromwell's New Model Army and on through history, involved the wives of the men who fought.

So it seems odd that marriage was for the most part discouraged in the army. Authority blew hot and cold on the matter. Soldiers fighting under King Billy in Ireland were allowed to marry, but not with Roman Catholics. Those under Butcher Cumberland in Scotland got into trouble if the bride came from a family likely to use information extracted from her husband to further the Jacobite cause. In some cases, men were deprived of privileges and even of rank on marriage.

Of course, the main and obvious objection was financial. Army estimates had to be made and accounts balanced. Official wives would be an official responsibility. Since the soldier usually spent the whole of his active life in the army, it was not to be supposed that he should be celibate, and authority made no objection to the droves of prostitutes that followed every regiment around. At a time when marriage was actually permitted but before much adequate provision was made for families, it was even suggested that those prostitutes considered suitable might be recognised officially and put through a course of religious instruction. Florence Nightingale, who got to hear of this suggestion, remarked that such an arduous life might entitle them to an army pension. These disease-ridden women represented a grave health risk, but nobody paid much heed to that. The soldier was considered a debased creature no decent girl would marry. "The uncontrolled licentiousness of a brutal and insolent soldiery", a description often misquoted, but all too often true, was made so by the conditions under which they lived. When "Other Ranks" were officially permitted to marry, it was only to the extent of four or sometimes six wives per hundred men. Nor can it have been easy to support a wife and the resulting family when in 1685 a colonel was paid twelve shillings a day, a major seven, an ensign three, a sergeant one and sixpence, and a corporal a shilling. Peculiarities of the army accounting system resulted in the chaplain being paid more than the surgeon, and the drummer as much as a corporal. A private drew eightpence only.

These conditions might have persisted had it not been for the Crimean War. This sorry campaign was the first to be reported and photographed, its scandals and muddles exposed by the Press. It came to the notice of the public that the soldier and his wife, human beings, existed in peace and in war under conditions worse than those of animals. Post-Crimean reforms resulted in a social upgrading of the army and the evolution of a ritual of courtship and marriage that seems with hindsight as bizarre as any tribal custom, which is, of course, what it was.

There was an enormous amount of snobbery in this ritual, inevitable in times when everyone knew exactly where they were with regard to social station. The rich man's castle might one day be invaded by the poor man at his gate, but as yet the rich man was hardly aware of it. In the army there was a well-defined and established hierarchy. At the top of the pyramid was the Household Cavalry, officered by the wealthy and well-bred. These were attendant on the Sovereign, and were followed closely by the Brigade of Guards. None of these regiments saw service abroad except in Egypt. Cavalry next, also rich but not necessarily as well-bred, though no officer would be accepted by the Colonel of the Regiment (not to be confused with the CO of a battalion) without the necessary social qualifications. The Rifle Brigade, the 60th Rifles, the two or three regiments considered the élite among the

Infantry, stood slightly above the rest, most of whom had equal status. All this was perfectly well known and accepted by army families who, like most professions, were inclined to intermarriage.

Girls living in garrison towns were in an enviable position owing to the plentiful supply of more or less eligible men of all ages. Mamma was even more conscious of this than the daughters, as was evinced in the old joke:

Q. What is a garrison town?
A. Mothers, daughters and the army.

The girls themselves were smugly aware that there was no need to search far and wide for dancing partners, and had no fear they would outgrow them in age as girls did students in university towns. Nobody minded being a "garrison hack" when there was so much fun to be had, with tennis parties, watching the man of the moment play polo or point-to-pointing, riding with him over Laffan's Plain and other places familiar to those who courted on horseback. Nor did the good time apply only to the army at home. Relatives or friends were bound to be stationed in Malta, Gib, or, best of all, India, and would be delighted to have Molly, Gwen or Peggy out for the cold weather. So the girls sailed joyfully away by P & O liner to join the "Fishing Fleet", see the Rock, the Grand Harbour, the Taj by moonlight, and find a husband. This practice was well-established long before it became part of army ritual and was a fruitful source of supply of wives for the Honourable East India Company. Lord Clive's wife was one of a party of young ladies who travelled unchaperoned for that very purpose.

Chaperons were, however, part of the courtship ritual right up to the Second World War. You joined a party with an older woman in charge for dances. For the theatre and cinema, mixed parties minus chaperons were sometimes allowed provided the parties were large enough and kept together. A girl had always to be careful "not to make herself cheap". This was a much emphasised injunction, though there was no qualifying explanation as to how it was accomplished. The brave spirits who snapped their fingers and went to restaurants and even night clubs à deux got themselves talked about, to the disapproval of mothers and the secret envy of the less go-ahead daughters. That young officers behaved what was called "honourably" on the whole was due to the fact that they were brought up to respect girls of their own class. What they did when feeling less respectful was a regimental matter conducted in places of established repute.

There were problems peculiar to this agreeable social structure. A girl whose father was in a "good" regiment might be asked out by an attractive man in a "bad" one. If she accepted the invitation, even without parental disapproval, her enjoyment would be halved by the guilty feeling of letting the side down. Daughters as well as mothers could become obsessionally regimental, referring to "our" and even "my" regiment and only considering marriage within it.

The greatest obstacle to marriage was money. An officer in a "good" regiment had private means, usually by allowance from his parents. As he was not permitted to marry till the age of 30, and in many cases was obliged to leave his regiment if he defied the prohibition, he had plenty of spending time and was usually in debt to his saddler, his tailor and certainly to his bank manager. Fortunately, there were various postings abroad he could apply for to cover the period necessary for financial recuperation. The King's African Rifles, the Transjordanian Frontier Force, the Somali Camel Corps and the Iraq Levies, were well accustomed to receiving dejected subalterns, whose pious hope was that no one richer would materialise in their absence to press on the finger of the beloved the diamonds they were unable to afford.

For the girl courted by the Other Ranks, life was no less amusing. Nannies and domestic servants in officers' houses had as much fun and as many strapping young men to carry on with as their social superiors. And nobody told them not to make themselves cheap!

Respectable civilian families living in or near garrison and depot towns did not look on marriages to non-commissioned officers with favour. The stigma of marrying a redcoat went on for a surprisingly long time. A young colour sergeant in the Royal Welch Fusiliers only succeeded in marrying his Irene on condition that if they were sent abroad in the near future the girl should come home for a month at the end of the first year.

Many girls had a tough and miserable time behind the scenes.

One wore an engagement ring suspended round her neck for several years until, at the age of 25, she wore parental resistance down. A ravishingly pretty girl of 17 married her officer and lived at home for a year without letting on. A Captain Kelly incurred the wrath of the Duke of Wellington by marrying a Portuguese girl against her mother's wishes during the Peninsular campaign. The Duke considered that Kelly had been guilty "of a gross breach of the laws not only of the land of Portugal but of his own and all civilised countries". Why there should have been so much fuss about this particular marriage is strange, as such cases occurred all the time. A courageous Spanish girl eloped with a drum major of the 88th regiment. Disguising herself as a cymbal player with a blackened face, she marched with the regiment under the eyes of her father, who failed to recognise her. Though this couple were married by a priest, there were repeated attempts to assassinate them as a revenge for her having married a heretic. Their happiness was short-lived, as the drummer was killed in action and his widow went back to her family.

For another Spanish girl, marriage with an Englishman presented no sort of problem. After the battle of Badajos, Juana Maria de Los Dolores de León, aged 14, bedraggled and with her ears bleeding from having had her gold earrings wrenched out by enemy soldiers, arrived with her sister at the tent of two young captains, Henry Smith and Johnny Kincaid, and asked for shelter (see p. 60). Both men fell in love with Juana on the spot, though Johnny was the more articulate. He described her as "an angel—more transcendingly lovely than I had ever before seen— more amiable than I had ever yet known". She married Henry, and was given away in a drumhead ceremony by the Duke of Wellington. With her Enrique, she soldiered all over the world, and 30 years later, her husband was to say that from the moment of their wedding she had been his guardian angel.

Engagements as brief as Juana's were unknown except on the battlefield. Three years was considered a suitable time for the young couple to get to know each other and save up to marry. Emily Allnatt waited that length of time for the Reverend Henry Polehampton, curate of St. Chad's, Shrewsbury. It was all *very* suitable. Emily was the daughter of a respected local family, Henry the grandson of a former much-loved vicar of the parish. The bridegroom was 32, the bride ten years younger, and with her marriage Emily's life would change entirely, since Henry had obtained an appointment as chaplain to the East India Company's troops, and they would shortly be setting out for Lucknow. It would be a double wrench for the Allnatts as their daughter Ellen was married to Henry Salt, serving with the Company's army. She was home at the time of the wedding, having brought her little boy to be left in the care of his grandparents. This child, Emily's godson, recalled in old age that "her beauty and gentleness endeared her to all who knew her; to none more than the nephew who recalls those times".

So it is as a gentle and beautiful bride that one may imagine her on that October day. Nobody present could have had any idea that gentle Emmie would become a bereaved mother, a widow and a heroine in the space of three short years, and that memorials recording her bravery and Henry's would be erected in the church where they plighted their troth.

Henry looked forward with eagerness to his new appointment. What Emily thought is not recorded. In a letter to his mother, Henry avers with the smug assurance of a Victorian husband: "Emmie takes it very quietly. I have no manner of doubt she will go where I do". The parish said goodbye to them with a silver teapot, and a purse of eighty guineas, both presented with a warm-hearted address by the vicar. The teapot was packed with the luggage marked "Not Wanted On Voyage", which went into the hold of the ship. Necessities for the long sea voyage were packed in trunks marked "Cabin".

So many thousands of wedding presents travelled that way, including of course the ubiquitous silver salver—the regulation wedding present from the Officers' Mess, engraved with the regimental crest and facsimile signatures of all subscribers. Drinks have been served off them in every corner of the British Empire, the signatures becoming a little less clear-cut as the years of polishing go by.

A favourite wedding present from an officer to his bride was a

1. Emily Allnatt, just before she married Henry Polehampton
(*By courtesy of* Mrs Maud Hamer)

jewel replica of his regimental badge. These, like the salvers, were
made to standard designs by the well-known firms of jewellers who
numbered the army among their customers, notably Garrards and
the Goldsmiths' and Silversmiths' Company. Crossed pennants,
grenades, guns, animals, cyphers, even a vegetable (the leek) glittered
in jewels and enamels, platinum and gold on the sporting felt hats
worn at race meetings, the wide-brimmed straws of Royal Ascot,
the satins and velvets of evening dresses. There were no official
presents from sergeants' or corporals' messes. Presents to army
brides tended to be of a practical nature "because you'll be moving
about so much". One sergeant's wife remembers with gratitude and
affection the mincing machine which fought the good fight with
ration beef from Wales to Gibraltar, Shanghai, India and back
again for all of 20 years.

Between the girl's acceptance of her beloved and the Wedding
March rendered by cathedral or village organist had to come the
permission to marry from the Colonel of the Regiment. This was
not necessary in the case of the Other Ranks, but woe betide the
officer who married in defiance of permission being refused. The
commanding officer of the man's battalion would detail his wife
to advise the regimental wives not to show any signs of friendliness
to the bride who was considered to have caused her husband to
disgrace his regiment. In some cases, the pressure caused the man
to exchange or even to resign his commission.

So there she was, the newly wedded and bedded army wife. The
girl from the manor, the cottage, the farm, the ancestral hall, the
city slum, the town house and the parsonage. Between the pages of
family albums she stands shyly beside her groom, surrounded by an
overpowering number of bridesmaids, one hand tucked into the
arm of her husband, the other clutching rather desperately at an
enormous bouquet; or posed stiffly in the local photographer's
studio, pillar and potted palm as background, her sergeant, his
waxed moustaches stiff as his ramrod back, staring fiercely into the
future at her side. Misty pictures by Lenare cause brides who have
long been grannies to wonder just when the slim creature in satin
became the stout party in tweeds, and why the pearls that gleamed
on satin seem so diminished in size on a larger lambswool bosom.

2. The wedding party of one Sergeant-Major Johnson, 40th Regiment, 1874. His bride does not look a day older than fifteen—perhaps she was a regimental orphan?

(By courtesy of the National Army Museum)

She would never have an easy life compared with her civilian sister's, but it would never be a dull one. She had embarked on a rackety over-the-hills-and-far-away life which she would never regret, provided she could find the one basic essential which all her sisters in all ranks sought—somewhere to live.

Before the post-Crimean reforms and when there were no regimental depots or barracks in garrison towns, the army was billeted in hostelries and lodging houses as it moved about and in semi-permanent camps when quartered in garrison towns. The officers made their own arrangements and were more or less comfortable. The wives and families of the Other Ranks were permitted—some of them, and provided they were "on the strength", (i.e. had not married below the permitted age of 26)—to live in screened-off corners of the barrack rooms. On the other side of the sacking lived anything up to 80 men.

Sanitary arrangements were non-existent and typhoid fever and tuberculosis endemic; the last brought about by the lack of any facilities for drying clothes when the men came in from sentry duty. The rough communal kitchens bulged with women elbowing each other for space in the greasy smoke-laden atmosphere. Behind some of the barracks, the men dug gardens out of disused ground to grow potatoes and greens, and kept a pig in a sty in the corner. An irritated officer remarked that nobody seemed able to stop them knocking shelves into their barrack corners, and it is evident that from earliest times the army wife showed her genius for snuggling down and making a home for her family wherever she happened to be.

The children born in these surroundings and who survived the experience ran wild over the barracks and the square, tough little gangsters dressed in cut-down uniforms or dresses made from their mother's almost-worn-out clothes. It wasn't a bad life. The un-married soldiers spoilt them, giving them tobacco and old clay pipes to smoke it in, and there was always a place in a warm bed vacated on Reveille. Bugle calls were often a child's first memory along with the clatter of hooves, the jingle of harness and the regimental ceremonial and tradition that made up so powerful a mystique. The soldier's family, and particularly his wife, lived his life to a remarkable degree. Not for her the kiss at the front door after breakfast and a day alone with the children till father came home at night. To live in or near to a barracks is to live in constant turbulence, unnoticed, undisturbed and taken completely for granted until comes the quiet of retirement and a constant nostalgia.

Married officers sometimes lived in barracks also. Major John Patterson, writing in 1840, describes one such newly-wed pair for whom "domestic seclusion is totally out of the question". The bride, "a promising young lady" soon "tamed down to a very languishing slipshod wife", disappointing her jolly ensign husband. There was no room for the piano, which had to be sent to the Quartermaster's Store, while the ensign and "the partner of his cares" stowed away as best they might amid the lumber of bed and furniture "very much after the manner in which steerage passengers are ensconced on board a packet ready to sail for Van Diemen's land". Despite these conditions, they kept a parrot and pretty birds in gilt cages till "the scene was changed and other little birds began to sing". Mrs. Ensign might have found time hang heavy on her hands, might even have envied the gossip and tittle-tattle that went on in the sudsy, steamy, communal wash house, where those wives registered as regimental washerwomen earned $\frac{1}{2}$d. per day per customer (in cases of heavy work, 6d. per item) for doing the laundry for all ranks. Everyone in barracks knew everyone else's business and for the soldier's wife, fisticuffing and feuding were as much part of daily living as the bugle calls.

Though the domestic life of the army was not reformed until the mid-nineteenth century, there were those concerned with their desperate condition considerably before that date. Chief among these was Captain Hugh Scott, 92nd Highlanders, retired, who, in two long and excessively wordy letters dated 1854, to Sidney Herbert, Secretary of State for War, referred to his gratification that the long battle he had waged was at last persuading an indifferent public to his way of thinking.

"It is admitted that the degradation of woman and the desecration of marriage are alike opposed to Divine and human law" he states in preamble, and continues "the argument which has been frequently employed against any amelioration for married soldiers is that you encourage them to marry, which is a serious evil for a marching regiment—we only propose to improve the accommodation for those married with leave—the moment you begin to stop what are called imprudent marriages you infringe upon the first principles of political economy and you create and foster immorality. Let marriage be allowed its fullest development and you can then operate a community and no sooner. Laws are only of use when they are supported by the public feeling of the community. When they violate it, they are so much waste paper. Orders in the army are necessarily imperative and without appeal—given out to be obeyed. When they are disobeyed and with impunity, they cease to be orders. The orders on the subject of marriage in the army are openly disobeyed by every regiment—if the present restrictions were removed, a higher class of woman would come into the army".

Two years earlier, Scott had issued a circular proposing the formation of a commercial company "for the purpose of building model lodging houses for the families of married soldiers. These would be in the vicinity of barracks and regularly inspected by the orderly officer. Good conduct and the regular payment of rent would be the test of admission, the children would be regular pupils at school and the wives attend Divine Service every Sunday. Cleanliness and tidiness were conditions of continuing tenancy". For this circular, he was censured by the Duke of Wellington as having committed a breach of the Articles of War. He remained undaunted, insisting that the difficulties in improving the situation had always been greatly exaggerated and the evils of the existing system minimised because of "a nervous dread that the soldier is to be more intelligent and of a higher stamp than he is—this is the phantom which flits before the fancy of the old stager. I feel convinced that should you devote your abilities to the solution of this social difficulty and persuade the government to put themselves at the head of a movement of this nature, you will commence a new era in the social history of the army, bestow happiness and comfort on many a hapless family and do much to raise the character of the British Army".

Scott's plans for lodging houses did not materialise, but when the soldier returned from the Crimea, he found himself a hero to a public that remembered what it had read of the appalling conditions in which his family had hitherto lived. This was the last war to which wives went with their men and their trials did not now go unnoticed. From the smoke of battle and the fire of public indignation rose new homes for the married families. Buildings of little architectural merit, they were revolutionary in their day: two storeys, divided into flats connected by balconies and with stairs at regular intervals. Rooms and windows were small, brick walls painted over without the refinement of plaster. A minimum of furniture included beds, a kitchen stove, cupboards and a living room with a table and chairs. Quarters were allotted to men married "on the strength" only. Those married without leave continued to live in grisly lodgings or in the collection of shanty-like dwellings that grew up round the garrison towns. The wife of the men's company commander visited all the company families, both on and off the strength, about once a month. Some looked on this as condescension, but by and large it was a good system which worked well. There was always pregnancy and childbirth to discuss, as everybody was within the age-range of both, and the officer's wife was expected to be the first on the scene with congratulation or condolence.

Married quarters were always full. Staff sergeants were all permitted to marry after the new reforms, 50 % of the other sergeants and 40 % of the Other Ranks. Permission for the last was only given after seven years' service, two good conduct badges and savings amounting to £5.

Officers' quarters were furnished with regulation tables and chairs, coal scuttles, fire irons and cupboards. The movable items were invariably slung to the back of any outside shed and forgotten till produced, at the end of a feverish hunt, for the Quartermaster, who had to take the inventory when the officer left. The commanding officers' houses, often built on to the end of the mess, were large and quite comfortable. Their architecture was mid-nineteenth century military, as distinctive of its kind as any non-conformist church or Victorian railway station. A CO was entitled to a soldier servant, a gardener and a groom. Other servants paid out of his own pocket would usually include a cook, a house parlourmaid and a nanny.

Many married officers preferred to draw lodging allowance and find their own accommodation. Before the Second World War, a four-bedroomed house, with three rooms downstairs and all the usual offices, plus garage and possibly stabling, could be rented for about £50 a year. The rates would bring it up to just under £100. If the wife had a bit of money, as was expected of her, there would be a gardener added to the other servants. An officer with large private means could live in state, running to a butler, while the poorer made do with a "girl" instead of a proper nanny. Generals lived in houses furnished by the Office of Works, with an ADC and an official chauffeur, paying for extra staff from their substantial allowances.

The great dread of the army wife of all ranks was unwanted pregnancy, which frequently seemed to occur at the mere mention of a move or a posting overseas, and which she would go to considerable lengths to terminate. Repeated doses of hot gin and quinine made the ears buzz and eyesight faulty, but were well worth it if they achieved the required result. Crawling upstairs backwards, jumping off a chair, riding hard to hounds, these and more sinister methods were well tried. One woman who lived to over 80 had no fewer than six pregnancies terminated in an Indian bazaar.

On the whole though, the army wife was a healthy creature, with a philosophic attitude to the ups and downs of her restless life. Partings from people and places when there had been just enough time to grow fond of them were little deaths over which she wept in secret before drying her eyes ready for the next adventure. In one particular, she was luckier than any other wife of any other man in any other profession. Never alone, never without friends, she travelled the world. She was sad, homesick, happy, ill or well in the company of those she knew and understood. It wasn't a question of liking or antipathy. Army wives belonged together in the mutual knowledge that their husbands were expected to give (and gave) first loyalty to the regiment, and that protesting about what they fancied to be their rights would get them nowhere. They could draw on a vast bank of shared experience and grumbling, funny situations and sad, partings and meetings. That bank was the whole archaic, traditional, violent, colourful institution that was the army into which they had married, and which ensured that loneliness was something they would never know anything about.

References to Chapter 1

The British Army by a Lt.-Col. in the British Army, Sampson Low
    Marston, 1899
Camp and Quarters, 2 vols., Major J. Patterson, Saunders & Ottley, 1840
Scenes and Impressions of Military Life, Major J. Patterson, Saunders &
    Ottley, 1840

*Letters to the Rt. Hon. Sidney Herbert on the present condition of married
    women in the Army*, H. Scott, Saunders & Ottley, 1854

2. Trooping

THE BRITISH ARMY transported itself, its luggage and its families over the world's face by many and devious means. The horse, the camel and the elephant drew its guns and the waggons into which was piled everything needed to sustain life in peace and war. All these necessities had previously to be taken across oceans, through storm and calm, under sail or steam, until ships were supplanted by the ubiquitous aeroplane. Families went abroad with the army as early as 1655, when General Venables commanding an overseas detachment of Cromwell's New Model Army landed his force in St. Jago, Jamaica. In 1703, Major St. Clair, an officer highly spoken of by Marlborough, had occasion to report on the arrival of the transport *Dorrell* at Ventry Bay in Ireland. The ship, which carried women and children as well as men, "had suffered loss of sail owing to contrary winds. Leaks are spoiling the bread and the ship is rotten".

Mary, wife of Corporal Robertson, RA, embarked with her two children to follow her husband into action against the French in Flanders in 1793. The ship carried no medical or surgical supplies and, added to this, the vinegar commonly used to wash and disinfect the decks had been omitted. Sir John Fortescue, remarking on this failure of administration, hopes that the health of Mrs. Robertson and the children remained good. There is no record that it did not, but if it did, they were lucky. Cholera was the nightmare on troopships. On one voyage, the state of the ship was so disgusting after an outbreak of this fearful disease that the soldiers set to and cleaned the whole vessel.

In 1773, Lieutenant and Adjutant Fred Mackenzie of the Royal Welch Fusiliers and his wife embarked on the *Friendship* for America, accompanied by their two children, Fanny and Gem. "A very old and crazy ship" Mackenzie says it was, with the cabin only seven feet square. There was no outside porthole and he had difficulty in opening the one small window that gave on to the cabin stairs. Afraid that they might die of suffocation, he kept them on the deck as much as possible. Three years later, at the evacuation of Boston, the army and its families embarked with all speed. Orders were issued that any woman found in the town after 1 pm would be left behind and baggage remaining on the wharves after 6 pm on the day of embarkation would be thrown into the sea. Rations for the families were meagre: "flour, rice and fish to be used with economy", in sharp contrast to those of the officers who enjoyed large regular meals.

One of the earliest, and very graphic, accounts of life on a troopship is left by Mrs. Sherwood, wife of Captain Sherwood, Paymaster to the 52nd Regiment, who travelled to India with her husband under sail in 1805. "Those who have not been at sea" she states flatly "can never conceive the hundredth part of the horrors of a long voyage to a female in a sailing vessel". The packet, an East Indiaman converted for trooping, does not seem to have been well adapted. The Sherwoods' cabin was situated close to the pumps and putrid water rose every four hours outside their cabin door. The walls were of canvas and their bunk was slung crossways over the gun. This miserable accommodation was shared with a Mrs. G., who was "touchy, hard to please and continually sick". Extra provisions were provided by passengers themselves, bought on land at a standard rate of £15 per head.

Mrs. Sherwood might have had even more to complain of had she been one of the party of three women and a child who accompanied their soldier husbands to Australia on a convict ship. Months at sea must have been more trying for Mrs. Sherwood than for anyone else, as she consistently disapproved of everybody and everything on board. Even changing for dinner was a waste of time as "I was the only lady on board who did not dance". A fiercely evangelical Christian, she read her Bible and kept her eyes open for the faults of others. She did, however, worry about the conditions under which the soldiers' families existed, and did what she could for the wife and children of her husband's soldier servant by insisting that they breakfasted with her every morning. The breakfasts were bad, but exquisite compared with what the soldiers and families got. The officers' wives, the ladies, were uncomfortable enough, but the wives of Other Ranks, the women, existed in inferno conditions below decks. No fresh air, no washing facilities except salt water in buckets, no sanitary arrangements except more buckets, no privacy by day or night in sickness or health, childbirth or death. And, over all, the stench of ammonia from adjacent stables.

Major Patterson waxes indignant over the accommodation for the ladies in 1840. "A state room!" he exclaims. "What a lying definition for such a wretched, murky, abominable hole, where there is every misery it is possible to think of or that it is possible to compress within the smallest space—an area of 6ft. square of dirty planks nailed up and tarred over". Major Patterson's opinion of troopships in general was poor. Anyone who went aboard "one of these rotten tubs" with "the smell, the darkness, the slippery decks and filthy lockers might as well be entering his coffin". Private Waterfield endured these conditions on the *Aboukir* in 1846, and his discomfort was enhanced by a fire which broke out following the inadvertent ramming of the *Aboukir* by the *Cressy*. The voice of an elderly woman on her way to live in Calcutta rang through the din of the ensuing panic as she marched forcefully about, commanding loudly "Soldiers, man the oars to keep her off".

It was not only on the high seas that ships were in peril. On May 16th, 1850, Assistant Surgeon Graham and 24 men, women and children of the Royal Welch Fusiliers were drowned in Lake Erie following a collision between the ships *Commerce* and *Despatch* whilst en route from Montreal to London CW. After the wreck and when the number of dead had been ascertained, coffins were prepared to receive bodies as they rose to the surface, which did not occur till June.

Three years later, Captain William Corbett, the 52nd Regiment, sailed for India on the transport *Barham*. Passengers were much annoyed on their arrival at the docks by the discovery that the ship had sailed early and they had to catch her up by steam tug. Captain Corbett, a talented artist, sent a drawing of the *Barham*, a sailing ship, battling in a gale and heavy seas, that must have struck fear into the hearts of his devoted mother and sisters. Letters home show him as enjoying the voyage. The weather for the most part was perfect, and the slippers his sisters had made for him most comfortable. That there were married families on board is evident from his comments on the wife of a Captain Campbell.

> Mrs. Campbell does very little but eat, drink and sleep on an armchair when on deck. She consumes a vast quantity of everything, I often catch her taking a back hander after dinner. Early this morning, I heard the chief officer go down to the Colonel's room and give him a flying fish for Mrs. Campbell's breakfast, and as soon as he had gone, I heard Mrs. Campbell say "don't you think, George, he could catch me some more, this seems a very little one".

Mrs. Campbell must also have enjoyed the voyage as they "carried a good cow, and there is a sheep killed every other day". She could begin the day well with a splendid breakfast, "ham, grilled bones, curry, muffins, liver and bacon, mutton chops, cold meat, marmalade etc." and keep up her strength with excellent claret daily and good port twice a week. It is a pity Captain Corbett does not tell his family of any part Mrs. Campbell might have played in the junketings to mark the crossing of the Line, when Neptune and his wife sat in a carriage rigged up from a gun and were attended by a doctor, secretary, barber, two bears, a policeman, a fiddler and a piper. The Captain was a prolific and detailed letter-writer, even to charting the wind and recording the weather. Against one such entry is the affectionate little addition "I wish, dear, you could have seen the sunset this evening, I never saw anything more lovely".

The Polehamptons (see p. 17) sailed for India on board the *Pera* in January 1856. Cabin accommodation had improved, but only slightly. They had bunks, under the mattresses of which all shirts and under-clothes, personal belongings and even writing cases had to be stored, as there were no drawers or cupboards. The rest of their clothes and belongings went under a berth in a small cabin trunk. The *Pera*, a new ship, part steam, part sail, ran into bad weather almost immediately and there was danger of engine failure. Henry did a calculation of the number of places per lifeboat and decided "how to act in the case of emergency and otherwise prepared for the worst". He instructed Emily and her sister Ellen Salt, who shared a cabin with her, that if anything went wrong, he would fetch them immediately, remarking that "they took it very calmly".

As Mary Anton (see p. 54) so often had "the tear in her eye" during the Peninsular War, so often does Emmie appear to have taken things calmly. The bad weather meant "fiddles" on the dining tables. "Mahogany frames are placed on the tables which stand up some two inches from the cloth. These frames are divided into little squares in each of which is room for a plate, tumbler and wine glass. Between the two rows of frames in the middle of the tables, the dishes and bottles are placed".

The calm that followed was disturbed by a death on board, an incident particularly upsetting for Emily and Ellen as the coffin was hastily knocked up outside their cabin. This being before the Suez Canal, they disembarked at Alexandria, went sightseeing in Cairo, and travelled six passengers per van, each van drawn by two camels and two horses, in 17 hours to Suez. It was a very comfortable journey according to Henry, who reported the party as being "very merry". At Suez, they boarded the *Hindustan* and had a pleasant voyage to Calcutta.

The post-Crimean reforms brought about the construction of specially-built army transports for the India run. By 1863, five of these were in use. They were served by officers and men of the Royal Navy, but such appointments were not popular. The standard aboard had been greatly improved to include proper cabins, nick-named "Dovecotes" for single ladies and those without children, while mothers with families shared larger cabins called "Nurseries". Husbands slept in dormitory cabins and had to help their wives with the chores, as there were no stewardesses. Real comfort was still a long way off. There was only one deck cabin which, during the heat of the voyage in the Red Sea, was allotted to officers' families by rota so that each could be assured of at least one night's cool sleep. There was an understandable uproar when a titled officer's wife insisted that the cabin was hers by right of precedence and that her child, being heir to a title, was of more importance than the children of other, less noble families.

Passengers who arrived safely and in a reasonable state of health at their destination after a long sea voyage could count themselves lucky. The India run was particularly dangerous, with the risks of capture by enemy ships, being fired on and shipwreck. Of these, the last was the greatest and all too common. Six women and 26 children were among the passengers who sailed for home from Ceylon in the spring of 1815 on board the *Arniston*. Mrs. James had her two children with her and poor Mrs. Taylor, recently widowed, was returning alone. The five-year-old son of a Mr. Gordon was travelling with his father only, so it is likely that Mr. Gordon had also been lately bereaved. The 14 soldiers' wives had 25 children between them, while Lord and Lady Molesworth had charge of the four little boys of Colonel Geilles of the 73rd Regiment, who, with his wife, remained in Ceylon. After a voyage of nearly two months, the *Arniston* foundered on Lagullas Reef, the southernmost tip of Africa, with the loss of all but a few of the crew and every passenger. The four Geilles children were buried together and a memorial erected to them. The bodies of the Molesworths were washed ashore locked in each others' arms. The small town on the point is named Arniston after the disaster. Charles Scott, the ship's carpenter, and his few companions made a signed statement of the facts on reaching Cape Town after great hardship on June 27th, but news did not arrive in England till October. It was published in *The Times* on the 27th of that month.

The *Birkenhead* had been specially modified for trooping and the modifications had deprived her of a number of watertight bulkheads. In December 1851, she sailed from Spithead for South Africa, carrying soldiers of eight different regiments as reinforcements for the Kaffir War. On February 26th of the following year, she foundered on a reef approaching Port Elizabeth, water flooding in all the faster because of the missing bulkheads. The ship was doomed from the first. All women and children were ordered into the cutters, the men had to fall in on deck. The whole scene was one of intolerable agony and horror, as the women clung to their husbands in what, except for a very few, was the last goodbye, and terrified blindfolded horses were driven overboard. The discipline of the men in these agonising circumstances was impeccable and heroic. Few of them could swim. When the *Birkenhead* broke in two and orders were given to abandon ship, it was impossible for all but a few to survive the dense seaweed and the waiting sharks. All women and children were saved.

3

The *Charlotte* foundered in front of the town in Algoa Bay in December 1854. By the light of fires lit on shore, the women and children could be seen imploring help. There was a heavy sea and the lifeboat was obliged to return to shore, having rescued only a very few.

The women and children aboard the *Sarah Sands*, an iron ship that caught fire after an explosion 400 miles from Mauritius, were all saved, after 24 hours afloat in the lifeboats.

Survivors of the Indian Mutiny, including Emily Polehampton and Lady Inglis (see p. 111), were wrecked off the coast of Ceylon on their voyage home when the Captain mistook a shore light for a beacon. The passengers all remained on board through the long perilous night till help came with daylight and the women were rowed 12 miles on the open sea to Trincomalee.

The *Eastern Monarch* was a fine ship, the best of all the sailing vessels that went between Great Britain and India. She had had a bad voyage between St. Helena and home, delayed by a persistent east wind which had caused her to run out of provisions, and the Captain put in at Spithead on his way up the Channel to collect meat and vegetables. An explosion occurred at 1.30 am on June 2nd, 1859. Everyone rushed on deck, the ladies terrified and shrieking in their nightgowns. Women and children were got hastily into the boats, though there is a grisly comment in a recorded account that "there was not room for all of them". Fortunately, two boats from a man-of-war came alongside and took off the remainder. The crew gave no assistance, and the fact that the loss of life was small was due to "the fortitude, humanity and discipline of the soldiers".

Possibly the last of the people who could claim to have been shipwrecked while trooping was Mrs. Margaret Kihn. She sailed from England as a child of five in 1888 and lived to be 88—her death was reported in the *Cape Times* on March 22nd, 1971.

With so many dangers to life and property involved in the long voyage round the Cape, it would seem surprising that the project to build the Suez Canal, which would more than halve the time taken, should have been greeted with dismay by the Peninsular and Orient Shipping Company and little enthusiasm by the British Government. But the P & O had large sums invested in its own

3. R.M.S.P. *Trent* at Malta, April 1854, with the Royal Welch Fusiliers for Constantinople
(*By courtesy of the Royal Mail Lines*)

wharves, offices and warehouses in Alexandria and in a hotel in Cairo. Farms on the outskirts of these cities which supplied meat, fruit and vegetables to the Company would be ruined; and the dues to be paid by the Government for the passage of troopships would be enormous. The project took ten years to negotiate and complete and in 1869 the voyage to India and beyond became a matter of safe weeks, instead of dangerous months.

From then on, trooping steadily improved, though there was still too big a difference between the accommodation of the ladies and the wives. The wives were below decks, their lives still pervaded by the stench of stable and what an officer feelingly described as "bouquet d'hommes". Once the Channel and the Bay of Biscay were left behind, life on a trooper could be very enjoyable. Food was plentiful and good, following the enormous menus traditionally thought up by the P & O. There were stewards, stewardesses, as well as laundry facilities—very different from the bad old days when Mrs. Sherwood had to provide all clothing and bedding for the entire voyage. The four-berthed cabins could be shared by a family or, in case of accommodation problems, by single ladies or two ladies with families, the husbands quartered elsewhere. The cabins were small with cupboards, drawers, a good mirror and washbasin with hot and cold. The water was salt, so it was necessary to use a special soap that would lather. Bathrooms were communal and the taps enormous, which could be a real danger. Many a wife, child or nanny turned on a tap to find that the water had been cut off, as it often was for mechanical reasons, and went away without remembering to turn it off again. The resulting flooding and the spoiling of a great deal of luggage always caused a lot of unpleasantness.

Entertainments were numerous. Many an old-age pensioner of today learned to play bingo under the name of Housey-Housey as a bride, and remembers St. Andrew's or St. David's Day celebrations in the Red Sea, where national and regimental traditions fought with flying fish and dolphins, high blue skies and stars as big as florins. A small memory shared by every wife who ever trooped is of handkerchiefs! Newly washed, they were pressed flat while still wet on to the looking glass or over the metal top that shut down over the

4. The wreck of the *Birkenhead*. She foundered on a reef off Port Elizabeth, in February 1852. All women and children were saved (A painting by Thomas M. Henry, *reproduced by courtesy of the* National Army Museum)

washbasin, so that they dried smooth enough to make ironing unnecessary.

Henry Wood's daughter, Olive, wife of Major Bernard Grissell of the Norfolk Regiment, was one of many women who said goodbye to ayah at Bombay knowing that she had to face the voyage with three children, the youngest of whom was still a baby. She herself was still feeling ill after a severe attack of dysentery. With luck, she would find an Other Ranks wife to help her during the day, and assist get the children to bed before the time came to dress for dinner (mess kit for the Major, lace and frills for his wife), one after the other as there was no room to dress together.

Well before the Second World War, troopships had become, if not luxury liners, at least very good indeed. The soldier of whatever rank was entitled to a free passage for his family and everything was free while on board for all ranks, including brands of baby foods. Drinks were paid for as in a Mess.

Some officers and their wives did not care for trooping and paid their own fares to travel by one of the private shipping lines. In 1903, a Mrs. Mitford took her three daughters and two maid servants to South Africa to join her husband, quartered in Pretoria with the British Army of Occupation. Although of a family of modest means, she declined to travel by troopship, having observed on a previous voyage goings-on of which she did not approve. As her daughters were still children, it is presumably the two maids who would have been at risk.

Trooping is over. The *Sarah Sands*, the *Birkenhead*, the *Riwa* and the *Somersetshire* sank in battle or were broken up in the scrap-yards long ago. The stoic, heroic women who brought their families alive and well to one end of the voyage or the other, or whose hearts bled as some small canvas bundle slid into the sea, are fading photographs in unlooked-at albums. The youngest of them are ageing women, whose grandchildren fly 20 hours to join their parents for the school holidays without turning a hair and to whom an improvised canvas swimming pool would be a bit of a giggle. The Sales, the Sherwoods, the Polehamptons, the Smiths and the Joneses, they had the best of it, though they may not have known it at the time. They never had to endure the alarming anonymity of the airport, for them every port of call was a hive of exciting strange activity: gully-gully men at Port Said; shopping in Simon Artz; accounts of mildly pornographic goings on brought back by the men from a night out before sailing; naked brown boys diving for pennies thrown over the side of a ship; half the workbaskets in the world bought for a few pence from vendors swarming on to the ship.

Who throws the coins now, or munches the incredibly sweet, incredibly delicious squares of Turkish Delight from Simon Artz, or gazes astonished at the Fuzzy Wuzzies, those strange, handsome men at Port Sudan whose extraordinary hair gave them their nickname? They have the even more extraordinary ability to stand on one leg for hours at a time. Who swims in the phosphorescent sea at Aden, the least beautiful body made beautiful by an outline of underwater diamonds? Who stands entranced by flying fish and jolly porpoises, and who, oh who, stands speechless on deck in the early morning as the ship passes islands gold, turquoise and amethyst in the misty early sunlight of the harbour of Bombay?

All this was common property to the army family. Many who saw these things as adults remembered them when the Fuzzie Wuzzies seemed taller and the gully-gully men a bit frightening. Many families trooped generation after generation. Major Henry Wood brought his young wife and two children home in 1866, returning after her death and his re-marriage with a new family. Of these, two returned to India, as did his grandchildren and great-grand-children, making a voyage, today seemingly as remote as any undertaken by the merchant adventurers, but then just part of their ordinary lives.

For one of Henry's grandchildren, the voyage home in 1913 held a sudden, sad moment, magical in retrospect. She stuck her five-year-old head through the rail to look down at the mysterious dark water, and the clasp of a string of bright blue beads broke, so that they slid without warning into the sea. And there they must still be, among the gold and silver and timber and bones.

References to Chapter 2

Following the Drum, Sir J. W. Fortescue, Blackwood, 1931
Troopships and their History, Col. H. C. B. Rogers, Seeley Service
Memoirs of Private Waterfield, R. Waterfield, ed. A. Swinson & D. Scott,
  Cassell, 1968

The Diary of Mrs. Sherwood, Mrs. Sherwood, Houlston, 1805

3. *Early Campaigning*

"To go". "Not to go". Terse little sentences that could spell life and death for a soldier's wife, as surely as if those were the very words written on the paper. For this was the ballot that had to be drawn every time a regiment was ordered abroad. It told four or, if they were lucky, six wives per company that they were permitted to travel with their men, and the rest that they must remain behind. The method of drawing lots was basic and brutal. "To go" was scribbled four or six times on pieces of paper, and "not to go" on as many more as were necessary to make up the number of wives. All the papers were put into the nearest handy receptacle—an old cigar box, a tin bowl, or an army cap. Then the door was opened to admit the first of the women waiting to learn her fate. The husbands waited with them, only too well aware that they faced the possibility of a separation of anything up to 15 years, if indeed they ever saw their wives again. This terrible system, instituted in the 18th century, continued till after the Crimean War.

It is not surprising, when one considers pre-Crimean military thinking and administration, that so few were allowed to go, or that women with children were not eligible for the ballot. The permitted few were only allowed to go because it was reluctantly conceded that women in restricted numbers had their uses abroad and on the battlefield. They were often the only nurses for the wounded, they cooked for their men and others, and they did the washing. Every woman received half a ration free, children over seven, a quarter, and under that age, a third.

But, as Captain Scott (see p. 23) pointed out in relation to the building of married quarters, many army rules were made only to be broken.

In the spring of 1776, Major General John Burgoyne sailed from Ireland—according to a diarist of the time—to "reduce the colonists (of North America) into submission to the British crown". This campaign, known now as the American War of Independence, was in contemporary accounts called the "War of the Revolution". In 1973, almost two hundred years after the following account of a remarkable army wife was written, it was discovered in a deed box in the strong room of a store where it had been deposited and forgotten at the beginning of the Second World War. The account is a copy of one written in Canada in 1777 by General Burgoyne, who had been greatly impressed by the heroism shown by Lady Harriet Acland during his expedition.

Lady Harriet had accompanied her husband to Canada at the beginning of 1776, and during that year had undergone with the troops the testing climatic conditions. At the beginning of the 1777 campaign her husband forbade her to go with him on the dangerous attack on Ticonderoga, but the day after Ticonderoga was taken he was badly wounded and Lady Harriet crossed Lake Champlain to join him. As soon as he had recovered she followed him through the campaign, according to Major General Burgoyne, in "a two-wheel Tumbril which had been constructed by the artificers of the Artillery, something similar to the carriage used for the Mail upon the great Roads of England".

Major Acland commanded the British Grenadiers attached to General Fraser's Corps. They were always the most advanced post of the army and had to be on the alert constantly, to the extent that often they all slept in their clothes. One night the Aclands' tent caught fire. Lady Harriet rolled clear, but Major Acland had to be dragged out by an orderly sergeant and was badly burned. All their possessions were destroyed in the fire. The accident happened a short time before the army crossed the Hudson River, and "neither altered the Resolution nor the Cheerfulness of Lady Harriet and she continued her progress as a partaker of the fatigues of the Advanced corps".

Another officer's wife, Mrs. McNeil, encountered danger of a different sort and had a less fortunate outcome from her adventure. Mrs. McNeil was related to General Fraser, and went with a girl named Jane McCrea to the British camp where Jane was to marry an officer. On their way, however, they were attacked by Indians and Jane was killed. According to Lieutenant William Digby, 53rd Regiment of Foot, in his journal, Mrs. McNeil was stripped of all her clothing and delivered to General Fraser "in a state of nudity", to the great embarrassment of the General "as his wardrobe was not provided with anything suitable for a lady to wear". How Mrs. McNeil overcame this great indignity is not recorded!

By 19th September the Grenadiers were expecting action at every step and the Major insisted on Lady Harriet's riding with the artillery and baggage which was not exposed to enemy fire. After the engagement had begun, Lady Harriet dismounted at a small hut which was soon requisitioned by the surgeon as a first-aid post. The place was well within earshot of the action, and Lady Harriet had to endure the din of battle, the sight of the wounded, and the knowledge that her husband at the head of the Grenadiers was in the thick of everything. There were three other women at the post: the Baroness of Riedesel, and the wives of Major Harnage and Lieutenant Reynell.

As it turned out their presence brought no comfort, for Major Harnage was soon brought in badly wounded, and Lieutenant Reynell was reported to have been shot dead. The small group of English women was deeply grieved; but Major Acland was unhurt and from that date until 7th October "Lady Harriet with her usual serenity stood prepared for new trials and it was her lot that their severity increased with their numbers".

On this occasion, again with Lady Harriet within earshot of the whole action, the British suffered a severe defeat and Major Acland was wounded and taken prisoner. Lady Harriet spent 8th October out among the wounded and dying, since no tent or hut was left standing other than those being used by the hospital. General Burgoyne was so impressed with Lady Harriet's "Patience, suffering and fortitude" that he allowed himself to describe her experiences in his account of the campaign.

I received a message from Lady Harriet submitting to my Decision a Proposal and expressing an earnest solicitude to execute it if not interfering with my designs of passing the camp of the enemy and requesting General Gates' permission to attend her Husband. Though I was ready to believe (for I had experienced) that Patience in a supreme degree were to be found as well as every other Virtue under the most tender Form I was not astonished at this Proposal after so long an agitation of the spirits exhausted not only for want of Rest but absolutely want of Food; drenched in rain for twelve hours together, that any woman should be capable of such an undertaking as delivering herself to the enemy, probably in the Night and uncertain of what hands she might fall into appeared an effort above human nature. The assistance I was enabled to give was small indeed. I had not even a cup of wine to offer her, but I was told she had found from some kind and fortunate hands a little rum and dirty water and all I could furnish for her was an open boat and a few lines written upon dirty and wet paper to General Gates recommending her to his protection. Mr. Brudenell the Chaplain to the Artillery (the same gentleman who had officiated at General Travers' funeral) readily undertook to accompany her with one female servant and the major's valet de chambre (who had a Ball which he had received in the late action in his shoulder) they rowed down the river to meet the enemy. But her Distresses were not yet to end. The night was advanced before the boat reached the enemy's outposts and the sentinel would not let it pass nor even come on shore. In vain Mr. Brudenell offered the flag of Truce by the state of the extraordinary passenger. The guards, apprehensive of treachery and punctilious to their orders, threatened to fire into the boat if it stirred before daylight. The anxiety and suffering were thus protracted through seven or eight dark and cold hours and her reflection upon that first reception could not give her encouraging ideas of the reception she was afterwards to expect. But it is due to Justice at the close of this adventure that she was received and accommodated by General Gates with all the humanity and respect that her Rank, her Merits and her Fortitude deserved. Let such as are affected by these circumstances of alarm, Hardship and Danger recollect that the subject of them was a woman of the most tender and delicate Frame and the gentlest manners, habituated to all the soft elegances and refined enjoyments that attend high birth and Fortune, by far advanced in a state in which the tender cares, always due to the sex, become indispensably necessary. Her mind alone was formed for such trials.

Major General Burgoyne devotes his account of the heroism of the army wife on this campaign to the misfortunes of Lady Harriet Acland, but she was not alone in her exhibition of bravery. Lieutenant Digby paid tribute to Anne Reynell in his journal of the campaigns. He writes that she followed her husband "so faithfully through the terrible scenes of the campaign . . . until the fatal 19th of September when he received his fatal death wound . . . she was left with three small children the oldest of whom was less than six years of age and the youngest an infant". These children were with their parents on this hard campaign.

A few days after the action at Stillwater where Lieutenant Reynell was killed, General Burgoyne wrote the following letter to Anne Reynell and sent with it a note for 50 guineas.

> Camp near Stillwater
> 24th Sept. 1777

Madam

As few officers carry in the Field more ready money than may be necessary for their immediate purposes I think it probable you may have some difficulty in this Point to add to a Distress that is sufficient of itself for all the Fortitude of human nature. A good mind like yours Madam will derive its first consolation from Resignation to the Will of Heaven. Permit me to request your acceptance of the enclosed as an assurance against temporary inconvenience and as a Testimony of the Sincerity with which I mean the more able Protection of Government the deserving Relict of a brave soldier.

I am, with the fullest esteem for your character and the deepest concern for your lot

> Your most obedient Humble Servant
> J. Burgoyne

It can be seen from these writings of General Burgoyne that the officers' wives accompanying their campaigning husbands were by no means ignored or uncared for, within the limits permitted by the situation.

The ineligibility of children to go abroad was one of the army's restrictions. All officers and NCOs loathed the ballot, and one at least owned to being reduced to tears by the agonising scene. In several regiments, it was put off till the last possible moment to allow an atmosphere of hopeful uncertainty to prevail, and to keep terror and grief at bay.

The fact that the terror was even more powerful than the grief shows the extreme poverty of the military family. The man had his uniform and a few personal belongings, the wife and children the clothes they stood up in, and a few cooking pots and pans. No home to pack up, no furniture to dispose of. Up and away, if you were lucky, and if not, what? If not, why then, dear God, the fate of the family left behind was terrible indeed. No provision was made at all for the wife or her children. Even if the man had been able to make an allotment out of his weekly pay of only a few shillings, there were no facilities for doing so. She must leave the barracks when the regiment left, making her way to wherever she wanted to go as best she might. If she was lucky, she might have parents who could and would support her.

If they were themselves too poor, or had thrown her out for marrying a redcoat, the only thing for her to do, before the days of the Poor Law, was to "go on the parish". This meant that the parish in which she had been born was obliged to give her a minimum of financial support, and, as their funds were always limited, they repudiated anybody they possibly could. Parish records of the 17th and 18th centuries are full of such cases, and soldiers' wives who had drawn "not to go" must certainly have been among them.

There are tragic and authentic stories of the adverse effects of the ballot. A sergeant in the Rifle Brigade, a man with an excellent record, cut his throat a few hours before sailing, unable to bear the knowledge of what his wife and child must endure without him. A soldier's wife, distraught, gave birth to a dead child in the street; and there is the terrible story of Duncan Stewart and his wife Mary.

The young couple were Scottish. Duncan's father was a farmer who grew barley for the making of whisky; Mary's, an exciseman. The natural antipathy between the two men made for a Montague-Capulet situation, which prevented the young couple who had fallen in love from meeting except in secret. When Mary discovered she was pregnant, they married in secret too. Soon after the marriage, Duncan was sent to a local fair with a drove of sheep, and took himself and his cares and worries into a tavern, where a recruiting sergeant was lying in wait for likely lads. He listened to exciting stories of the military life through a thickening haze of whisky, and remained just sober enough to accept the King's shilling. The sergeant marched him off to Edinburgh and signed him on. Before poor Duncan was really aware of what had happened to him, he found himself with his regiment at Hythe.

It was three weeks before he finally managed to communicate with Mary, who had been distracted with wondering what could have happened to him. Near her time though she was, she set off at once to join him. The happiness of reunion and the possibility of a life together was short-lived, as after one week the regiment was ordered to sail for the Peninsular War. Came the ballot. And Mary drew "not to go". She stood there, reading and re-reading that awful message without a word. Then she fainted. Some kindly wives of other soldiers left behind to form a depot kept Mary inside at the moment of march-off, but she rushed out to Duncan with a scream that curdled the blood of all ranks present and implored everyone, anyone, within earshot, not to take her husband away.

"Poor Duncan", says a contemporary account, "stood all this while in silence, leaning his forehead on the muzzle of his firelock and supporting his wretched wife upon his arm. He shed no tears, his grief was evidently beyond them", though men, from officer to private, who witnessed the scene were weeping. Then he spoke to Mary. "You may come as far as Dover at least" he said, and gained for her a few hours', a few miles' reprieve. The column began to move, band playing and the men shouting and singing, partly to demonstrate their own good spirits, partly to drown the screams of the women left behind. Mary walked beside her husband, but it became clear all too soon that her anguish was physical, as well as emotional. She was hastily taken into a wayside cottage, where she was received very kindly.

Duncan was allowed to remain with her on condition he rejoined the regiment as soon as possible. He stayed long enough to see his Mary die and to know that their baby, delivered by a hastily-summoned doctor who performed a posthumous caesarean operation, drew two or three breaths only before it joined its mother. Duncan reported to the regiment and refused the compassionate leave offered him to attend the funeral. He asked for assurance that his wife and child would be given decent burial and, having received it, he embarked for Spain in dumb, uncomplaining despair, being himself killed within a short time of landing.

Perhaps Mary's fate was not so much worse than that of some among the 120 Canadian wives stranded in Portsmouth, when the regiment in which their husbands served was re-ordered overseas within a very short time of returning from Canada. Their struggle for survival in a strange country must have been grim. Stories like these, and more, would have circulated among the army, and strengthened the resolve of every wife "to go" whether she drew lucky or not.

And go they did, by fair, foul, or any other means, contravening the regulations and, as often as not, getting away with it. Officers were human beings and Lord Nelson was not the only one to put a telescope to a sightless eye. Many an odd-shaped bundle was loaded on to the transports without any inquiring what was inside. There was the young wife who blackened her face and marched in the regimental band, and was not recognised even by her own father, and the snobbish Fanny Duberley, who disguised herself as a regimental woman, in an old shawl and battered hat, to be smuggled on board the *Himalaya* sailing from Varna to the Crimea.

Some women actually fought as soldiers to be near their husbands. Two wives are mentioned as having done so in Cromwell's New Model Army, and Mrs. Christina Davies, who went to war in 1692 in an effort to find her husband, made such a good soldier that her sex was not even suspected till a wound necessitated surgery.

By 1706, the advantages of having women in the field or in foreign countries were again discounted and attempts were made to stop their going. When these proved unsuccessful, some effort was made to care for and accommodate them on the transports. A comparison is made between the expense of an expedition under General St. Clair in 1702 and one that was to succeed it. In both cases the ratio of women to men is the same, 583 women to 5,012 men (evidently a number of "not to go" wives managed to get themselves smuggled on board), and 200 women to 2000 men, indicating that the regulations had been strictly observed on the second expedition.

The first expedition consisted of 25 transports, store, baggage and victualling ships and a hospital ship. Judging from the estimated cost, the second expedition would have consisted of 12 or 13 ships. The cost of feeding was the same on both occasions. Fifteen shillings and threepence was allowed per month for men and women alike. Mentioned under "incident charges" are "one hundred and thirty eight officers' cabins at six and sixpence each, five thousand four hundred and fifty private men's cabins at four shillings each, at the cost of one thousand and ninety pounds". One of the more expensive items to be taken aboard was 20 tons of vinegar, at a cost of two hundred and six pounds ten shillings. This was a necessity: the only disinfectant available at that date, it was used for scrubbing the decks.

Having endured the discomforts and considerable risks of ocean travel, the wife could expect no betterment of her lot when she touched dry land again. The Duke of Wellington disapproved of wives in the field, and before him General Wolfe testily remarked that there were far too many at Quebec. Their leather stays and petticoats drying on the branches of trees offended his military sense of dignity and propriety. The wives in this campaign had official rivals in the "sutlers", or "settlers" as they were sometimes called. These were women who followed the army and sold provisions. They never achieved the status of the French vivandières, though they do appear to have worn some kind of uniform in the shape of a linen skirt and woollen cap. It may have been these caps that defaulting soldiers were obliged to wear while standing for an hour outside the latrines as part of their punishment drill. The wives, too, were threatened with punishment on occasion. An order was issued that if they persisted in selling liquor and making their husbands and others drunk, they would spend the remainder of their time in Canada locked into the holds of the ships.

Home once more, many of the same wives set out again, this time for Spain. Tougher, more weather-beaten, harder drinkers and swearers, they carried the same few belongings in bundles and a child or two added to the existing brood trailing at their heels. It seems that their number was now officially increased and they numbered 20 and even 30 per company. Captain Johnny Kincaid, of the Rifles, observed one woman marching with 1100 men, but

4

as he was, on at least one occasion, declared to have written his
accounts of campaigning with undue levity, this may have been an
exaggeration.

The Peninsular War had a distinct social side to it. Officers'
wives and families made prolonged visits to Lisbon, which was much
more amusing than London or their country homes, and where there
was dancing, riding and flirting with heroes. There was also gossip
and scandal over various attractive young wives left behind at
Lisbon when their husbands went off to battle. Mrs. Scobell, wife of
a major, kept a good table at which Mr. F. S. Larpent, the Judge-
Advocate General, often dined on "tender fowl and mutton". These
were pleasant little dinners, with no other ladies to rival the hostess,
who liked to reign supreme. After dinner, they would gamble at the
game of loo. Mr. Larpent also spent an agreeable Christmas Day as
the guest of Colonel Campbell, in whose house he always enjoyed a
good dinner and, just as important, "the best society". Since many
regiments spent six years in the Peninsular, it is not surprising that
life under war conditions became the norm. Many of the younger
officers had known no other. It was mostly very comfortable and
vastly entertaining.

No comfortable lodgings, no flirtations in scented gardens, hands
meeting and clasping through the softness of kid gloves, the
emotional rise and fall of a bosom barely concealed by satin or lace,
for Mrs. Mackenzie and the other wives. It would be interesting to
know their opinion of the ladies. Wives knew their regimental place
and kept it, even though they knew about the carryings-on of the
ladies.

Not that all wives were virtuous, far from it. Theirs was a different
kind of morality, largely brought about by the sheer necessity to
survive. A girl who accompanied 1100 men was a practised pick-
pocket, and must have taken a nice little haul with her when she
deserted to the enemy. An army chaplain had the poorest opinion of
the wives, considering them "as bad as any soldier in licentiousness
and crime, doing nothing but harm to any army on foreign service".

Within a specified radius orders were issued that no woman
might buy bread. This was an attempt to stop them ranging far and
wide, stealing fruit and vegetables wherever they could and traffick-

ing in wine, which they were not allowed to bring into camp. The women were, if anything, more drunken than the men, and a disgusted observer recorded seeing a party of them standing waist-deep in wine in a cellar they had discovered while on one of their foraging parties. In extreme cases of disobedience, a woman could be flogged. This did not often happen, though the Duke of Wellington was severely censured for allowing it. On one occasion, several of them were formed up and got "sax and tharty lashes on the bare doup".

Silks and satins and wasp-waisted riding habits for the officer's lady; torn red jackets and cracked boots, stripped from the dead, for the soldier's wife. The knapsack, also plundered, on her back had often to be emptied of its miserable contents to accommodate a new-born baby. After a Mrs. Robertson had given birth to the latest of her several children, she had to walk many miles, following the column; and she was one of many. Whether this did any lasting harm or not, and painful as it must have been at the time, it was certainly better to be within range of other women's help, of food, and a certain amount of husbandly concern. Not that poor Mrs. Robertson got much of the latter. The sergeant adopted the customary nonchalant attitude to her, to the children, and to the fact that a recent stroke of ill-luck had caused them to lose all their belongings.

All soldiers' wives are only too familiar with this attitude. What the wife doesn't like, she must lump. If she gets too grousy, there's always some duty her husband can go on, or the protective womb of the Mess. So Mrs. Robertson and all the others plodded on, often going ahead of their husbands on the march to be ready with a cup of tea brewed on fires of sticks gathered wherever they could find them on the way, the water from the nearest stream or river boiled in the kettle which was as necessary a part of the wife's equipment as ammunition was of her husband's.

Biddy Skiddy, a stalwart woman, carried her husband when he declared himself exhausted on a long march. Sergeant Skiddy, a good soldier, declined to part with his knapsack, so she shouldered that too. If she had been the one to drop in her tracks, she would have received no such kindly treatment from him. It was not permitted for soldiers to quit the ranks to help a woman.

There is a more cheerful picture of the journey of an officer's family following Wellington's column. The lady rode a horse, holding up an umbrella against the hot Spanish sun in one hand, and in the other, the reins and the lead attached to the nanny goat, acquired to supply the milk for the infant son who travelled in a pannier on one side of a donkey, balanced by luggage and equipment stowed on the other side. The soldier's wife, employed as his nurse, walked alongside. A small dog sustained a precarious position on his mistress's lap.

Children struggled and trotted for miles, keeping up with their mothers and the army. Whenever possible, they were smuggled on to the baggage carts, hidden under sacks, tents and mounds of equipment, scrambling out if there was likelihood of discovery, since such indulgence was strictly against regulations.

Wives on the march had more to do than keep themselves and their families alive. After every engagement, it was they who searched the battlefields if their husbands were missing, bringing them in if wounded, trying to secure them decent burial if dead, and comforting the widows. Someone would in turn comfort them when the dreadful need arose. Sometimes a woman, crazed with grief, had to be forced away from the body of her man.

Afterwards, she and his orphans had somehow to be fed and cared for till she could take up the thread of daily life again. The plight of the woman widowed on the battlefield was desperate, since from the moment of her husband's death her right to any rations for herself and her family ceased. There were only two courses open to her: to depend on the charity which her friends could not long afford to give, or to remarry, which she often did with all possible speed. In return for food and a basic security, such as it was, she gave her new man the care she had given his predecessor—his food, his hot tea and comfort in the cold ditches that were often their only bed at night.

The highest number of husbands acquired by one woman in the Peninsular War appears to have been six, her last being a man named Gilbert Hinds. The fact that the marriages were of necessity and not lightmindedness is borne out by the fact that she lived with Hinds faithfully to the end of her life. As Private Metcalfe (see p. 194)

5. This was how the army travelled in 1802, and for nearly a century afterwards (Drawn by W. H. Pyne, *and reproduced by courtesy of the National Army Museum*)

that cheerful diarist, would have said 50 years later, it is hoped they were happy.

Most of these women were truly magnificent, and at least one is known to have been killed by enemy fire while helping a wounded soldier. Some became brutalised and callous and refused help to the wounded, but they were few. For the most part, they were cheerful and encouraging to their men and to each other, making light of their own discomforts, like the wife who so impressed Colonel Augustus Frazer of the Royal Horse Artillery when he met her and her husband making a slow and painful journey to Lisbon in an attempt to apply for the blinded soldier to be invalided home. The man, in spite of sightlessness making the going extremely difficult, carried his two-year-old daughter in his arms, while his wife carried the five-week-old baby (born on the battlefield) and guided her husband at the same time. Their lot was the harder as their donkey, which the wife in common with most of the rest of her kind had managed to buy, had been stolen, so that they had to carry anything they possessed in the way of luggage. Their cheerful acceptance of their situation so amazed the Colonel, and aroused such instant respect and admiration that he made arrangements for them to be sent home at once by sea. Many women fell dying on the way, desperate, alone and abandoned, like the girl whose lifeless body was found by the roadside, her new-born baby groping blindly for her cold breast. New-born twins, found naked but living by the side of their dead mother, were discovered by a posse of soldiers who kept them alive till they were handed over to women willing to care for them.

For a day-to-day account of married life in the Duke of Wellington's army, history is much indebted to Quarter Master Sergeant Anton, of the 42nd Royal Highlanders. Anton was a tough son of an equally tough widowed Scottish mother, and joined the militia in 1802 with £15 put by in savings, which he had increased to £60 before joining the 42nd. This was an almost unheard-off feat for a lad in his position, and all the more remarkable in that he sent his mother a sovereign at regular intervals. Anton was canny. He knew exactly where he was going and who was going with him. He chose Mary, a plain, sturdy, peasant girl, as shrewd as himself, who could drive a bargain and knew both sides of every penny before she parted with it. They were a splendid and endearing couple, devoid of Scottish dourness, and they made the best of every situation, enjoying many of them enormously.

Anton, always articulate, was particularly strong on the necessity for improving the lot of the soldier's wife. He pointed out that the selection of wives without children to follow their husbands abroad was no doubt best from the army's point of view, but that the deserving woman "thus cast on the public, or left to her own exertions, which too often fail her, in her endeavour to support herself and children" became a burden. "I am no great theorist" said Anton, with slight understatement, "but I am certain that much might be done to obviate the necessity of soldiers' wives being burdensome to the public by adopting proper means for their support". He advocated the institution of marriage allotments to be made by soldiers serving abroad; he considered it disastrous that the army child had no real conception of the word "home", "welcome sound to the ear of the cottage boy to whom it brings to mind all the pleasant recollections so firmly impressed on his mind that age is incapable of effacing them".

Anton was a fulfilment of the saying that as the twig is bent, so the branch will grow. Mary, though she had much to endure following the drum, was always assured of the happiness and security of affection from her husband, who had received these from earliest childhood, and of a home, however makeshift, to enjoy them in. Anton considered that the wife of the private soldier had as much right to go with her husband as the wife of the NCO, and that "she will prove much more useful than one who, instead of being serviceable, considers herself entitled to be served and helps embitter the domestic enjoyment of others by exciting petty jealousies that otherwise would never exist". He had a poor opinion of these superior wives who, he observed, get more than their fair share of the rations by being insistent, to the disadvantage of the younger women too intimidated to protest.

Having arrived in the Peninsula, Mary Anton spent her first night in a tent with her husband and 17 other men. They lay all through the uncomfortable hours till morning, 38 feet to the pole in the middle, 19 heads crammed against the skirting flap, the bodies in between piled high with knapsacks and accoutrement because there was nowhere else to put them. "Often did my poor wife look up at the canvas that screened her face from the night and wish for the approaching morn."

Dermatitis, brought about by bad conditions, was rife among the soldiery and this and the discomfort of that night made Anton resolve "if possible, not to mix blankets with so many bedfellows again". So they built themselves a hut which, with the help of friends, they finished in a day.

This was not an uncommon practice among the married men with wives sufficiently refined to wish for a place of their own, but certainly none made themselves more warm and cosy than the Antons. The hut was very small. Anton, not a tall man, could stretch the whole length of it lying down, but it was their own and private, with a door made from Mrs. Anton's apron, pins serving for locks and and hinges. Anton records with gratitude that not a man attempted to enter as long as the door was shut and they never had the slightest fear of anyone doing so during their absence. It was summer time and the living was easy. Then came the autumn and heavy rain. They moved to a new, larger hut on higher ground above Urdach. Anton dug a trench round the outside to take the water from the roof and soak it away and, as a protection against the high winds, he threw a blanket over the hut and pegged it down. But during one violent gale which blew up in the middle of the night, the branches that supported the roof collapsed and fell on their heads. The blanket was swept away and most of the roof too, so they crept out and into the shelter of an overhanging rock, while all around them they could hear the shouts of men struggling to re-pitch their blown-down tents. Anton was on duty on advance picket two miles away in the morning and Mary, left alone, collected a few branches and "huddled them together" over an open umbrella to make some sort of shelter. All their provisions had been blown away, so she left their new and very temporary home and went to try and buy bread. It was lucky that she had money, for the price was high, but she bought some and also wine, and set out to take them to her husband who had had no time to collect anything after the disastrous night.

With her limited resources, she could not make much of a meal, so she mulled the wine in her kettle and added the bread to it. Hurrying along, she slipped down a steep bank "and rolled down a considerable declivity", spilling all the lunch. Unhurt, but very upset at the waste of time and food, she hurried back, bought more, mulled and mixed all over again, and set off for the second time. "The tear was in her eye" says Anton, using the delightful expression peculiarly his own, "as she related the misfortunes of the day, but she returned to camp gratified at having provided me with unexpected and comfortable refreshment".

Anton and his Mary were a cheerful, level-headed couple, who cared deeply for each other, managing through their combined resourcefulness to make themselves what Anton calls "the most comfortable of the uncomfortable". Over the building of their third hut, he describes himself as "a regular Robinson Crusoe when regimental duties permitted". He borrowed an entrenching tool from his friend Fraser and dug a widish trench three feet deep inside and another four feet deep round the outside of the hut to carry off the water from the roof.

Writing his memoirs in later years, he remembers with gratitude "the indulgent manner in which I was treated and for not being troubled with vexatious interruptions". One can only suppose that this was due to the Antons being a couple universally liked and respected for their industry. Friends willingly gave their assistance, digging, building and finally thatching the hut with bracken leaves gathered on the nearby hillside. They were unable to pay for labour, so Mary carefully hoarded a drop of spirits from her husband's daily allowance. When she had accumulated enough, they all had a drink together. At the end of two weeks, the hut was finished, snug and watertight, with the final refinement of a fireplace at which they sat eating their evening meal on the night of November 9th, 1813, blissfully happy at having a home. But even as they ate, the drums outside beat "orders" and Anton learned that camp was to be struck that very night.

The tear was doubtless in Mary's eye and in Anton's too as they looked upon their bower of happiness which Anton describes as "my little habitation, my sole property", in unconscious echo of that homesick poet who wrote of his village in sixteenth-century France and wonders:

> Quand reverrai-je hélas de mon petit village
> Fumer la cheminée? et en quelle saison
> Reverrai-je le clos de ma pauvre maison?

While Anton's hut was built by himself, du Bellay certainly did not build his beloved home "at the expense of a blister on every finger". Blisters and all, Anton "exulted over it in secret as the rich man in the Gospel did over his extensive possessions and his plentiful stores". He could not bear to burn it down, as others did, so they moved on and left it standing and the embers on their hearth grew cold.

Winter set in and life grew harder for everybody. A woman less lucky than Mary was the poor soul who had made some sort of a home for herself and her husband in a disused pigsty, only to be evicted while her husband was on duty by a single man who disliked the greater discomfort of his tent. Mary Anton kept up with the column on the march very well, except on one occasion when her donkey refused to cross the River Ardour and she was in danger of being left a long way behind. A passing grenadier picked up the donkey, a mere colt, and carried it over the bridge, Mary following. As she thanked him, the tear was in her eye again.

The retreat to Corunna was a fearful ordeal for the women, comparable to that from Kabul 40 years later, a withdrawal undertaken in much the same conditions of starvation and intense cold. The confusion was such that a military chest containing £25,000 had to be hurled over a cliff to prevent its capture by the French. The wife of the master tailor of the 52nd Regiment clambered down with considerable temerity and climbed back again, her pockets stuffed full of gold. Later, on embarking at Corunna, she fell into the water, the gold weighted her down and she drowned.

Many died, their names forgotten, their sufferings blown away on the wind of war. But some are remembered, like Sally Macan. She lent her garters to an officer to bind what remained of the soles of his boots to the uppers, and received his thanks a year later, when he was able to give her a lift on his horse after she had given birth to a child in a bivouac. Rifleman Harris tells of Mrs. Pullen, captured and raped, her son of 12 sent as a prisoner of war to France. Another woman to be captured and never heard of again was a Mrs. Howley. There must have been something very remarkable about her, for, according to Captain Grattan, she was mourned by the whole of the Third Division, "Perhaps in the entire army another woman, take her for all in all, as Mrs. Howley could not be found". As is usual in war, the enemy behaved on occasion with kindness. Among the stories of murder and rape are others, equally authentic, of tents being pitched, food and wine provided, guards mounted and captives returned unharmed.

General Baird's cook, though nameless, goes down in history as a termagant, who tried to turn out some officers and men when, half-dead with cold, they were thawing out by her kitchen fire at the moment she arrived to get the general's tea. Whether he was terrified of the good cook or badly wanted his tea is anybody's guess, but he sent his ADC to evict the intruders. Fortunately everybody, including the cook, had a last-minute change of heart and they were allowed to remain.

Nelly Carsons, wife of Captain Grattan's soldier servant, got so drunk one day that her husband, not knowing what better to do, bundled her into his master's bed, where she went to sleep. While Carsons was out, the Captain was brought in wounded and Nell's drunken slumber was too deep for her to be roused. The only thing to do was to shove her to one side and lay the Captain down beside her. Someone remarked that it would be a bit of comfort to have some warmth alongside him. On waking, Nelly quickly pulled herself together and made tea and while she and Grattan were drinking it, Carsons returned with three sheep and a pigskin of wine he had looted. The Captain found the whole situation so hilarious and laughed so much that his wound began to bleed in an alarming manner. A surgeon had to be sent for to stop the flow.

There were one or two cases of bigamy, and a sergeant, whose wife deserted him and their children, found that she had married a carpenter. He tried to persuade her to come back, but ended by giving her new husband sixpence before saying good-bye for good.

Mrs. Reston and her four-year-old son had a narrow escape when a shell from a 24-pounder hit the faggot she was using for a pillow. A woman of action, she shoved her little boy into a nearby bomb-proof shelter (one of the first occasions this amenity is mentioned). It was, however, already occupied by two women having hysterics, so Mrs. Reston set about giving a hand all round. She helped the surgeon dress wounds and a terrified drummer boy to draw water from a well under fire. Then she helped repair the battery, took her turn in handing on the ammunition and eventually carried all her own and her husband's luggage and equipment to the boat when the time came to abandon Cadiz. This remarkable woman survived all her adventures without a scratch and died in 1856, having been for many years a nurse in the City Hospital, Glasgow.

It is on record that on more than one occasion, women actually helped rout the enemy, so perhaps the army regulation that no woman might beat a soldier was more necessary than it might seem to be. Some ladies rode in front of the army, like Mrs. Dalbiac, who rode at the head of the 4th Dragoons, exposed to constant fire and showing no sign of fear, or Mrs. Mackenzie, who rode a white charger in the reteat from Corunna, not in the least afraid for her vulnerability on so conspicuous a mount.

The army wife who always prospers, and can sometimes cause her husband to prosper too, is the one with a pretty face and manners, who takes trouble over older men. Such a one was Mrs. Currie, wife of General Hill's aide-de-camp. She was always invited to adorn his dinner table as "a fair beautiful Englishwoman, a charming representative of those bright stars of Albion". She played the part of heroine in the many theatrical performances hastily organised whenever possible to entertain the troops and presented an enchanting picture at balls held in farm buildings, barns, or anywhere with a floor at least not dangerous enough to break an ankle.

But brightest in the galaxy of women on the battlefield shines the Spanish bride, Juana Smith (see p. 17). It was a tremendous partnership, hers and Harry Smith's, a mating of eagles that lasted for life. At the age of 14, she had already experienced the horrors and hardship of war, her wounded brother having died in her arms. Juana Smith cared not a rap for the hardships of military life. All that mattered to the girl from the high-born home, educated in the seclusion of a convent, was to share every minute of her life with her Enrique. She could neither talk English nor ride, but learnt to do both very quickly.

The slow, reliable mount Harry bought for her did not suit her at all, so she graduated to Tiny, a much more interesting ride. When the horse slithered down a slippery bank, crushing Juana's foot and breaking a bone, it was obvious to everyone that she must remain behind until the foot mended. It was not in the least obvious to Juana. She would ride a donkey, which must be procured at once, or better still, a mule. A Spanish lady's saddle would do very well, as her foot could be supported by the platform stirrup.

Harry was busy with brigade duties and had no time to devote to domestic responsibilities, but there was a score of devoted admirers to scurry round. By the time he returned, the whole affair had been resolved in exactly the way she wanted and he gave up trying to protest then or ever. Not that he was a henpecked husband, far from it. It was simply that he had complete trust in his wife over every-thing she did. Even the fact that she was so much admired, not to say adored, by his brother officers was a source of pride to him. This unique treasure was his, and his alone, so he could afford to pity those others who were her slaves and who got no favours in return except laughing thanks.

For her part, Juana was well aware that many other women around her were more beautiful than she, and that her Harry was handsome and vital and attractive. She had no cause for the jealousy she sometimes declared she felt and Harry knew the claim was made in fun, since she was as certain as he himself was that this was the only woman he would ever love. It was her warmth and gaiety, her large sympathy, her fearlessness, her acceptance of and adaptation to any situation which involved her personal discomfort and danger, that made her an acknowledged heroine among all ranks. In cold, hunger, discomfort and pain, she simply laughed and everyone who heard the laughter was cheered by it and adored her. The soldiers liked her to ride with them, a compliment paid to few, if any other women. Major Smith's wife was "a good soldier". Hard to under-stand, mind you, with her few words of the lingo, but that didn't matter when there she'd be, marching alongside when the going was too bad to ride, stumbling along, her habit soaked and heavy with rain and mud, leading her horse and that little pug of hers—Vitty, she called it, short for Vittoria. Some wounded French officers had given her the dog after she had been kind to them. She'd be kind to Boney himself if she thought he needed it. Come to think of it though, she must have given the Major many a good fright scampering about the way she did. But she thought a rare lot of him, no doubt about that. She did indeed. Enrique was the sun, moon and stars in her sky.

The only times she ever lost her head, and nearly her sanity, was when she thought Enrique had come to some harm. There was the terrible time when she was watching the fighting from the window of a cottage in which they were billeted, and saw Harry's charger, Old Chap, shot down and Harry disappear into the mêlée of wounded and dying. Frantic, she dashed out of the cottage to find and bring in the dead body, to discover she had been mistaken. It was the Spanish colonel, Algeos, on quite a different horse, who had been slain. Poor man, poor man, but thank God it wasn't Enrique.

Then later, she heard that her husband was killed in the Battle of Waterloo. In vain did West, the faithful groom who never left her side in Harry's absence, try to prevent her setting out at once to find his body. West would make inquiries, he would go to the battleground himself. Madam must stay where she was till he got back. It might be good news. They did not know for certain that the Major was dead. Ah! but she did know. They had told her. Nobody would have brought such cruel news if it had not been true. They would go at once.

And go they did, riding among the dead and the dying, dismounting in terror and dread to turn over a lifeless body wearing Rifle green, stumbling against shapes that moved and groaned, hearing the sobs and wails of women whose search had ended, terrified that at any moment, she might be holding Harry's lifeless head against her breast, while he gazed up at her from sightless eyes. And then the miracle happened. Someone found her and led her back to where Enrique was alive and well. The arms that clasped her were strong and living, the heart beat with life and love. He was alive! Thank God! Thank God!

Her story has been told many times because it is so worth the telling. She belongs to legend as well as to history, established in her rightful position at the head of that column of women, known or nameless, who followed "Old Hookey" alongside their men, living and dying like them during the long years it took to drive Boney over mountains, plains, rivers and finally the sea to St. Helena.

Sometime during the battle of Waterloo Colonel William Verner, 7th Hussars, was startled by what he described as "a rough voice" upbraiding somebody with the admonition, "What's the matter with you? Are you afraid?". Turning to see who it was and why they seemed to be playing the coward he saw to his astonishment that it was a woman who was being thus addressed. Riding a small pony, Mrs. Edwards, wife of a sergeant-major in the 7th Hussars, had followed her husband everywhere since the beginning of the campaign. Now, like Uriah the Hittite (though for a very different reason) she was about to find herself "in the forefront of the hottest battle". Captain Fraser, to whose troop the sergeant-major belonged, pointed out that a wife could hardly go into action at her husband's side "and", says Colonel Verner, "ordered her immediately to the rear".

After the final victory of Waterloo came the scramble to get home. No more living in huts and ditches, no more spicing stolen wine in tin kettles to keep the cold out. The days for plundering were gone. The next child would be conceived in a feather bed with sheets. Good-bye to mud and filth and hunger, and good riddance. And what was it like when you got back? A bit dull?

Stories of granny's adventures would be handed down and down, woven round the bits and pieces all wives brought back and treasured. One of the most unwieldy of these must have been the hub of the wheel of a gun-carriage. Mrs. Vear had been delighted when her husband presented her with this gift while still at war. It was just what she needed to stand the flat iron on when she was ironing the laundry of the several officers she worked for. She used her iron stand for years after she got home, by which time it had historical and sentimental as well as practical value. But, alas, the day came when Mrs. Vear's great-great-granddaughter found the thing ugly and useless. She threw it away, casting it into that limbo of past treasures which had become too much trouble to dust and for the loss of which society is so much the poorer.

But not all came home after the victory. The British army of occupation remained in Europe for three years. During this time Sergeant Edward Costello, the Rifle Brigade, was one of those who married French girls. His bride, Augustine, was the daughter of well-to-do French peasants, and because of their opposition the marriage was kept secret. The poor girl was left behind when the sergeant returned to England, but managed to join him at Chatham so soon that her unexpected appearance astounded her husband. Their circumstances were not easy. Augustine gave birth to a child soon after her arrival, and Costello was due to go before a Board to obtain his discharge for wounds. While awaiting this discharge they "struggled with our necessities" on sixpence a day. Costello was awarded £5 blood money for wounds received at Waterloo, but no back pay for those received in the Peninsula. The couple reluctantly decided that Augustine must return to France since the sight of a grandchild would certainly reconcile her parents to the marriage. They travelled together by way of Dover and Calais as far as St. Omer, and from there Costello returned home, helped by a fellow-mason who gave him a free sea-passage. The story ends sadly with the news of Augustine's death a short time later.

So the army came home, and life went on. Death came to the Emperor on St. Helena, riches and honour to his victor, who became Prime Minister to the nation of shopkeepers Napoleon had failed to conquer. It was 40 years before women went to war again.

References to Chapter 3

The Autobiography of Sir Harry Smith, H. Smith, John Murray, 1910
Cromwell's Army, C. Firth, Methuen, 1962
A History of the British Army, 7 *vols.*, Sir J. W. Fortescue, Blackwood, 1899–1912
Random Shots of a Rifleman, J. Kincaid, Boone, 1835
Retrospect of a Military Life, Sgt. Anton, W. H. Lizars, 1841
Short History of the English People, J. R. Green, Dent, 1960
The Subaltern, G. Gleig, Blackwood, 1825
Waterloo, J. Naylor, Pan, 1968
Wellington and his Army, G. Davies, Blackwell, 1954
Wellington at War, A. Brett-James, Macmillan, 1961
Wolfe at Quebec, C. Hibbert, Longman, 1965

Letters and Despatches of John Churchill, First Duke of Marlborough, John Murray, 1845
The Private Journal of F. S. Larpent, Judge-Advocate General, attached to Headquarters of Wellington during the Peninsular War, from 1812, ed. Sir G. Larpent, Richard Bentley, 1853

4. The Crimea

DID FANNY DUBERLEY think of Juana Smith as she rode with the army in the Crimea nearly 40 years later? And did Juana, Lady Smith, now wife of the Governor of Natal in South Africa, with a town in the Province named after her, ever hear tell of "Mrs. Jubilee"? It is likely they would not have cared much for each other had they met. Fanny would certainly have resented sharing her honours of war with another woman, and to the high-born Spaniard the flaxen-haired daughter of a country banker might well have appeared provincial. But they would have had memories and experiences to share, since each endured an entire campaign.

Fanny had two consuming ambitions; to ride splendid horses and to marry a cavalry officer. In both she succeeded—or very nearly. Henry Duberley, a nice, dull, rather lethargic man, was not strictly speaking a cavalry officer, but he was paymaster to the 8th Hussars and presumably Fanny reckoned that that was as near as she was likely to get. They had only been married a very short time when Henry was ordered to the Crimea with the regiment, and Fanny, 25 years old and very strong and healthy, packed up and went too. From the moment of their departure, she kept a journal and wrote frequently to her sister, Selina, and the result is a lively and interesting account of one woman's war.

She got off to a poor start, as the weather was bad and she was acutely sea-sick. Added to her misery and discomfort was her anxiety as to the condition of her two horses stabled in the hold of the ship. As soon as she could get out of her bunk, she insisted that Henry took her down to see them. On the way to the stables, she passed through the accommodation below decks in which the women and children were battened down for the whole voyage in conditions worse than those endured by the horses, which had grooms to look after them and were fastened by head ropes and slings in bad weather to save them buffeting and injury.

Nobody cared for the women. The berths and hammocks were far too few in number, so those not practised or determined enough to grab them at the outset slept where they could. Rations and water were short and often tainted, and there was no sanitation except for a few buckets. The ammoniac smell of horse urine seeped upwards through the boards, to mingle suffocatingly with the stench of unwashed bodies, human excrement and gin.

The first woman to be a Crimean War casualty met her death in quarters such as these. Mrs. Parsons perished in the fire which broke out on board the *Europa*, not far out of Plymouth. On the other hand, the wife of a sergeant in the Coldstream Guards gave birth to a child while Fanny was fussing about her horses, and both she and the baby survived to thrive. Horses were not the only animals aboard. Cows had to be carried to supply milk, and sheep to provide meat. Fanny did not notice the discomforts of the women in passing, but she was distracted over the welfare of her horses. Her grief at the death of her favourite, a grey, was such that she could never bring herself to mention him or even to write his name.

The Crimea was the last battlefield to which women went with their husbands, and the first to be fully reported and photographed. Roger Fenton from London was the most famous of the photographers, but there were others whose names have never been officially recorded, among them Ensign Henry Wood of the 30th Regiment.

There are women whose names are remembered with pride for the services they rendered in the Crimea. Mrs. Longley gave valuable assistance to the surgeons and was herself wounded. Momentarily leaving the wounded to the care of others, she searched the field of Balaclava after the battle and found her husband's dead body. A lancer helped her make a coffin and together they dug the grave to give him a decent burial. As a widow, she devoted all her time to nursing. Almost immediately after her return to England at the end of the war, she went as a nursing volunteer to India, where she worked during the Mutiny. Home again, she worked at King's College Hospital and subsequently remarried. Initially, she should never have been out in the Crimea at all, as she had drawn "not to go" in the ballot, but she sought the help of Lord John Russell, the

Whig leader, in whose family she had been employed, and he obtained the necessary permission for her.

Mrs. Elizabeth Evans (see p. 75), wife of Private Evans, an officer's servant in the King's Own Regiment, was a woman of outstanding beauty, as well as strong character. For her, the regimental colours represented everything for which the King's Own fought and died and she never let them out of her sight, marching as near as she could keep to them in spite of hideously sore feet. She kept up appearances, not for show but because it was not in her nature to lower her high standards, and she even managed to secure a modicum of privacy for herself and her husband by means of a curtain strung across the tent where they slept at night. She was very particular about her dress, looking stylish even when wearing articles of clothing sent out for the troops, which she accepted not out of greed, but necessity, since she was literally in rags. And, whenever possible she wore an attractive bonnet, made and trimmed by herself. Of all the hardships of war, she most disliked the fleas and being left alone without her husband at night. She waged a constant, if only moderately successful, war against the former and refused to submit to the latter in any circumstances. On the nights when "Soldier" was on night picket, she insisted on joining him and not all his protests could induce her to go back to camp. She made herself responsible for the regimental laundry and for caring for the regimental colours, repairing them when necessary. Other regiments than her husband's were known to leave their colours in her safekeeping in moments of sudden emergency. Miss Nightingale heard such good reports of her and of Mrs. Box (tall Becky Box, always able to find a drop of brandy for a tired soldier) that she appointed them nurses in Balaclava.

None of this meant anything to Fanny Duberley. She was having a splendid time entertaining officers in the leafy bower she had had constructed alongside her tent, while she amused them with her wit and responded gaily to their admiration of her golden curls and her horsemanship. Copies of the photographs Fenton took of her were distributed among the admiring soldiery, who gave her her nickname. She tirelessly talked on her favourite subject with that superb horsemaster, Captain Nolan, and rode with the Earl of Cardigan,

6. Fanny and Henry Duberley—a picture taken in the Crimea by R. Fenton. *(By courtesy of the National Army Museum)*

Commander of the Light Brigade. Cardigan, not accustomed to con-
ceding favours to ladies, was so bewitched by her company and so
overcome by her tears when she learned that Lord Raglan had
refused permission for her to travel to the Crimea with her husband,
that he agreed to turn a blind eye to any efforts she made to
do so.

Being Fanny, she laid and carried out her plans successfully,
which is how she came to be witness of the Charge of the Light
Brigade on October 25th, 1854. She had Henry to thank for this
experience, since he summoned her to the scene with a brief note
that has become famous, delivered to her tent early one morning. It
read: "The Battle of Balaclava has begun and promises to be a hot
one. I send you the horse. Lose no time but come up as quickly as
you can". Then, knowing his wife's enormous appetite, he added,
"Do not wait for breakfast". As she galloped up to the cavalry
camp, Fanny was actually under fire from a few random shots. It was
a beautiful autumn day. The heat of a summer which had scorched
the turf over which Fanny and her admirers loved to ride, dried the
thyme and rosemary that smelt so sweet in spring, and set men's
throats on fire with burning, hideous thirst, was over now. The sunlight was tolerable and the nights blessedly cool. One strange thing
was noticed, which brought sinister memories to those who had
served in India. Vultures, birds hitherto unknown in the Crimea,
came from no-one knew where and settled huge, scrawny, hideous,
on the rocks, waiting.

Women other than Fanny watched too: Mrs. Evans, Mrs.
Longley, Mrs. Davies, Mrs. Polley and nameless others, straining
their eyes to try and keep track of their men. Relatives too, mothers
come out to be near their sons, and sisters, and the tourists who came
out for fun. For this was a package-tour war and Messrs. Inman, an
enterprising shipping firm, ran cut-price trips: fourteen days' travel,
accommodation, visits to the battlefield and Constantinople at the
inclusive rate of £5. One family, travelling in the care of Lord
George Paget returning to the front after leave, took such mountains
of luggage that he had to hire a brewer's dray to convey it to the ship.

What did the army wives think of the tourists, some of whom wore
the newly-fashionable crinoline, seated round their baskets of cold

7. "The Return from the Crimea"
from the painting by Sir Noel Paton, RSA

roast chicken, while servants opened bottles of champagne? It is a wonder they were not set upon by the ragged, hungry women, but there is no record of anyone having even thrown a stone. Waiting women, waiting vultures. Time was suspended as they watched the frightful, fatal, mismanaged charge, unable to understand what had happened, what went wrong. And then the aftermath. Wounded brought in, dying left where they were for lack of men to move them, women searching for the dead, the vultures scuttling nearer and nearer.

Fanny returned to the Earl of Cardigan's yacht in which she had a cabin and spent a nightmare-haunted night. "I slept, but even my closed eyelids were filled with the ruddy glare of blood". She had lost many friends, including Nolan, but Henry, thank God, was safe. Not that he had ever been in danger. Being a non-combatant, he had taken no part in the battle. Fanny would genuinely have been distraught with grief had he been killed, though there seems little to explain why, in this strange partnership, anyone as vivacious should have been so devoted to anyone so dull. She was very much shocked by the slaughter of Balaclava and felt ill for some days, but her bounding health, high spirits and famous appetite soon brought her back to normal and she began to enjoy life again, a life that still offered male admiration and horses. Men, horses and excitement, these were the air she breathed and she took great gulps to restore her.

She had little use for women, with the exception of her sister and Lady Errol, wife of Lord Errol of the Rifles, who commanded the First Division and whom Fanny tried to cultivate without much success. Poor Lady Errol. No green-lined tents and leafy bowers for her. She shared a tent with his lordship and since there was only one bed, and she was the dutiful wife of an officer who needed his sleep, she slept on the floor. When the tent collapsed in a violent gale which blew up in the middle of one night, Lord Errol was extracted by some soldiers from the engulfing wreckage and her ladyship struggled out by herself, clad only in her nightgown. This beautiful, aristocratic, elegant woman did not respond to Mrs. Duberley's snobbish advances, but she gathered up the rifles of men too exhausted to carry them any further and hung them anywhere she could on her horse and herself, and encouraged her maid to do the same, as they rode among them towards Sebastopol.

Amidst all the macabre hurly-burly of this war, the muddle and the mistakes, the slaughter and grief, the gasps of the dying and sobs of the bereaved, the enmity between those in high places and the frivolity of the tourists, moves the strange luminous figure of Lady George Paget. This girl of 22, the bride of her cousin Lord George Paget who commanded the 4th Light Dragoons, exercised, without apparently making the slightest effort, the most magical effect on any man she met. Lord George had to leave for the Crimea soon after the wedding and so greatly did he pine for his love that his depression became a byword among his brother officers. His longing found expression in one of the tenderest, silliest and most endearing requests ever sent by a soldier at the wars to a wife at home. "Go to Gunters", wrote Lord George, referring to the fashionable London confectioners, "and eat an ice cream and think of me while you are doing so".

From the same front a private soldier, who had probably never heard of the Pagets, as they had almost certainly never heard of him, picked a flower and sent it home to his girl with the same sentiment. "I send you this flower which I have picked on the heights of the Alma. When you look at it, think of me". The girl from the village could not go out to be with her lover. The bride from the high-born world could, and did.

Lady George Paget caused a greater sensation on her arrival in the Crimea than anything Fanny could ever have aspired to. It is not surprising that Fanny disliked her, dismissing her with condemnation for being a bad horsewoman. Nor was she famous for her conversation or wit, nor in fact for anything except that extra quality, a sort of shining light that dazzled all the men she came in contact with, from Lord Raglan, the Commander-in-Chief, to wounded drummer boys, and all the other soldiers she visited in the hospital tents. So potent was the spell she cast that the men begged for "a touch of your ladyship's hand" as she passed by. She had to be requested to be sure and visit every tent, as those who heard she had been but had missed them out fretted to an extent which caused them physical harm. The Austrian-born Commander-in-Chief of

the Turkish army thought her wonderful, and the Italian general
who arrived with an expeditionary force was beside himself with
excited admiration.

She watched the Battle of Sebastopol from her horse at Lord
Raglan's side, and when the fighting was over, General Sir John
Pennefeather cut the medal from the coat of a dead Russian soldier
and pinned it on her shawl. Her friendship with Lord Raglan brought
light and at least some degree of happiness to the unhappy man,
whose heaviness of heart daily increased. When he lay ill in the
farmhouse that served as his headquarters, news of the progress of
his illness was brought to her every day until on June 28th, 1856, his
staff gathered in the farmhouse as he lay dying and she hurried to be
with him. They made way for her as she entered, to kneel at the foot
of the bed and so remain till the broken heart of Lord Raglan, worn
out with striving to accomplish a task too hard for him, ceased to
beat. Her husband, standing among the watchers, remembered the
vigil kept by the golden-haired girl in such strange conditions,
commenting later and with truth, "a curious event it was, a lady by
the bedside of a dying commander-in-chief in the field". Agnes herself died in childbirth two years later before age could wither "nor
the years condemn".

So much has been written about the horrors of the Crimea in
reports sent home from the field, and in letters that alarmed parents
and families, that it must have been a relief for the family of Ensign
Henry Wood to learn from his own hands that he was enjoying himself. "My dear Father", wrote Henry in a letter headed "Camp
before Sebastopol", July 29th, 1855, "I am very glad I came out
here and shall stay as long as I can. We all wish that something
decisive would happen and that we might take the field, for now it is
monotonous to the last degree. One day out of five is passed in the
trenches, the others in perfect idleness, excepting for regimental
work, which is not much out here, and a working party, which is for
twelve hours out of fifteen days. The principal amusements are riding about, bathing, either in the Ternija or in the sea, and in the
evening there are always bands playing".

This "perfect idleness" resulted in race meetings, dinner parties
and balls, which provided a full social life, fuller and more social than

Fanny Duberley at least would have led at home. Young ladies came out to visit brothers and have a good time, of which a battle was a tiresome interruption. Ensign Wood tells his family about trench duty.

I dine at 5 pm and at 6, the men fall in with their rations for the next day and march to the parade ground, where each regiment is told off to its place in the trenches, and at 6.30, they all move off. The officers ride as far as they can, for everybody here sports a beast of some sort, and they are also provided with provender. I take a biscuit and chocolate and strong tea, also cloke and waterproof, for the weather is never to be trusted and though the temperature is ninety three in a double tent at midday, one's teeth chatter often towards the evening. We ride about a mile and a half, as far as it is safe to do so, and then it is about the same distance to the advanced trenches. As soon as we get to our place, the old party leave, generally under a smart fire for the Russians know the time of relief as well as possible. As soon as it is dark, sentries are placed along the parapet, and if you have the end of a trench, one or two double sentries are placed beyond it, they lie on their bellies and have to keep a sharp look out. You then pick out a soft stone and so the night is passed, relieving sentries and keeping the men awake being our principal amusements, varied every now and then by grovelling on our stomachs to escape a shell.

He goes on to recount an adventure that his family would sooner have not known about:

I had rather a lucky escape last time I was on. We were in one of the most advanced trenches that had only just been made and was merely a row of gabions, with a little earth thrown on the other side. I had been sitting for some time, leaning against one of them, and had only got up for a few seconds to watch the firing from a mortar a little way off when a shell from a Howitzer struck the very gabion I had been leaning against bursting and wounding a man on each side. I never had been so much shelled as on that night and the constant cry of the sentries to "look out" and our efforts to make ourselves as much like pancakes as possible effectually prevented sleep.

It can be seen from these descriptions that Mrs. Evans must have had a chancy time, dodging her way under cover of dark to join her husband. Morning found them "filthy objects", covered with dust thrown up by bursting shells, but "in comparative safety, for sorties are not made by daylight. By six o'clock in the morning, the sun is burning. They now provide us with sunshades, made of canvas and fixed on firelocks. The flies are intolerable and in the evening, a few stray mosquitos come out". When the relief arrived at 9 p.m., "one is not sorry to leave. The men get out of the trenches as best they can by any dangerous places and form up afterwards. I have my horse to meet me. So much for the trenches. A wash sets me all right again. You never enjoyed such a wash. I eat a tremendous dinner and tumble into bed".

No horse to meet Mrs. Evans, no hot water to wash in, unless she drew and heated it herself, and no comfortable bed in which to sleep off her meagre supper. But she did wash the dust away, one may be sure, and spruced herself up to look smart and pleasant to men who liked to see a woman taking a pride in herself.

The war ended and the peace treaty was signed on March 31st, 1856. There had been a round of positively hectic social gaiety towards the end, and no doubt many of the visitors were sorry to go home. With the army went the tattered colours, the laurels of bravery and the rosemary and rue of bitter memories. Fanny Duberley wept for friends laid in their graves, beautiful Agnes must surely have grieved for Lord Raglan, and Ensign Wood found the head of a Russian soldier, soaked it in lime to burn the flesh away and took the skull home as a present to his family.

The transports bringing the army home docked in Portsmouth on April 11th, and the Queen and Prince Albert reviewed the battered, bearded men as they marched past the royal party on the parade ground. For Fanny Duberley, this was to have been a moment of triumph, as she sat on her horse, the only woman among the veterans, while the Queen and her Consort walked up and down the lines. Now she would be compensated for the fact that Her Majesty had declined to accept the dedication of her journal by being greeted on parade. But no. A very slight inclination of the head and royalty passed on. Snub. No medal, though everyone who knew said she deserved one. Even Lady George, who could not sit a horse properly had had one of a sort, though it had belonged to a dead Russian. No recognition of the fact that she had sustained the whole campaign and that the Earl of Cardigan had been among the many who acknowledged her magnificent horsemanship and her courage! Nothing but a little leave, riding over the quiet Wiltshire countryside with dear (but dull) Henry, remembering times when her Bob had cantered beside the Earl of Cardigan's magnificent Ronald and she had laughed and talked with his glittering rider.

Then back to regimental soldiering in Ireland, which was to prove expensive enough to oblige them to seek a posting to India, a step most officers in "good" regiments avoided taking on social, as well as health, grounds. But in the end, Fanny can claim to ride in the fore-front of all army wives, for she went to war again, riding with another column and into another battle, while for all the rest of them cam-paigning days were over. The struggle had been won on their behalf for better quarters, better welfare, better conditions. No need for suicide born of despair; no babies born in ditches within the sound of gunfire; no families subsisting at starvation level on the parish. Whatever the disgrace and maladministration of the Crimean War, this lasting result was a good one. It liberated the army wife into being a *person* with a right to bear her husband children and to have conditions in which to bring them up as human beings.

References to Chapter 4

Colonel's Lady and Camp Follower, P. Compton, Hale, 1970
Florence Nightingale, C. Woodham Smith, Constable, 1951
Mrs. Duberley's Campaigns, E. E. P. Tisdall, Jarrolds, 1963
The Reason Why, C. Woodham Smith, Constable, 1953

Little Hodge: extracts from the diaries and letters of Col. Edward Cooper Hodge written during the Crimean War, 1854–56, ed. The Marquess of Anglesey, Leo Cooper, 1971

5. *India*

GENERAL JOHN JACOB (1812–1858), one of the dedicated, almost mystical band of soldier-administrators known as the Bayards of India, once delivered a devastating opinion in no uncertain terms. If India was won by the sahib, he feared it would be lost by the memsahib. She had no part to play in India. She would never acclimatise herself and boredom would cripple her character, while the sun ruined her looks. If he was right about the majority, and there is no doubt that he was, the minority most certainly proved him wrong. Nowhere in the British Empire did its women and children endure more suffering than in that great continent where everything from the sun, moon and stars to history itself is outsize.

The story usually began joyfully enough with a wedding. On such a day in 1795, Delia Brown "from a quiet village in Gloucestershire was married to the gallant youth of her choice, under whose protecting care she had agreed to go to the Far East and seek her fortune". Alas for new-found happiness! Young Mr. Turner died less than a year after they reached Calcutta, leaving his widow with no means of returning home. It took a year before the letter of sympathy arrived from her parents, brought "by a fine handsome young artillery man called Claxton". Fortunately, "they day by day became much attached, and when he received orders to go up country, they married in Calcutta".

Life opened up for her under a new name. As a soldier's wife, Delia moved with her husband to Agra, where she bore her husband a son and the daughter named Delia who was his special favourite. The children's health was an anxiety and little Delia's papa personally superintended the prescribed cure for her debility; a glass of sherry after every meal. Education was also a problem, until the battery sergeant offered to be her tutor, finding his pupil particularly adept at writing and accounting. He also taught her to sharpen and mend her own quill pens, a habit which she continued all her life. A favourite amusement was riding with her father. After the siege of Bhurtpore in 1826, the child of 11 rode among the ruins while he explained "all the attack and the mine arrangements to her". The Claxtons had saved for years to return to the England their children had never seen, but when the time came, it was discovered that the bank which held all their savings had failed. They were obliged to return to Agra, where Major Claxton died not long afterwards, Mrs. Claxton following him a year later. The younger Delia's early education stood her in good stead during a life that included three marriages and as many widowhoods, as well as the managing of one of the most important British-owned estates in India.

One of the least endearing of officers' wives must have been Mrs. Sherwood (see p. 29). Like Paymaster Duberley, Sherwood had chosen a wife who could leave him standing with regard to energy and character. Mrs. Sherwood differed from Mrs. Duberley in one important respect. She was ardently and evangelically pious, and censorious with it. In her opinion, every Indian should be converted to Christianity. Until this happened, the whole country would remain a vile, stinking sink of iniquity. But she has left through the medium of her tract-like stories a valuable social commentary on the military India of the 1840s. A journey home from Cawnpore to England yields several interesting and, one would think, unusual details about passengers and friends. Mrs. Burton "took a dram extraordinary one afternoon, fell overboard and was never seen more". Charlotte James got no further than Patna, where she eloped "with a young spark of a civilian in whose acquaintance she had before fallen". Between Patna and Bar, the river-borne boat ran into a heavy squall and a sergeant and his wife went overboard. She was pulled out of the water and revived, only to fret herself to death over the loss of her principal piece of luggage: a chest containing all her clothes and bonds and securities for money. "Had she laid up her treasure in heaven", the writer remarks, "this would not have happened", adding with smug and not quite warrantable assurance, "I have always found that godliness is profitable both in this world and in the world to come". Poor Kitty Spence was briefly glimpsed in Calcutta, where she had been sent for trial for the attempted murder of a fellow-wife. She had escaped hanging, but refused to return to her kind husband and escaped into the city to live with some low-class whites.

The voyage from Calcutta was bad and often rough, and Mrs. Dawson was buried at sea, having died of drink. Nelly Price got into bad company on board and when they docked at Portsmouth, decided that a certain way of life was more congenial than the poverty and hardship in England. Many of the returning families landed in a sorry state. Having spent all their money in India, they arrived in England "in white muslin gowns, coloured shoes, trailing and shivering along Portsmouth streets".

No doubt the soldier's wife was a very tough nut. Fights were conducted in the barrack rooms in full view of everybody and egged on by the men. Drink was nearly everybody's besetting vice and wives not only consumed it, but sold it at a profit when they could get it cheap. Mrs. Paddy Burns, wife of a man in the King's Own Light Dragoons, did a very profitable trade with her Tin Baby; a barrel with a wax face wrapped in a shawl. She would take it into the canteen in the evening, fill it up with more than a gallon of grog at an anna a dram and round to the barrack rooms, where she sold the stuff at four annas a dram. But these women, rough as they were, cared for their men, in hospital and on the march, when deaths from cholera and fever were all too common. One party of women were the victims of a hideously sick joke, when the body of a soldier laid in too shallow a grave was disinterred and dismembered by jackals. Some of his mates picked up his severed, bloody head and chased the women with it. "They did scrawl out", remarked Sergeant Pearman, recounting the incident in a letter home.

Women whose husbands died followed the usual practice of marrying again as soon as possible to avoid going "off pay", which unhappy state overtook them six months after widowhood. Orphaned daughters as young as 14 were married off too, since a widowed mother had no means of supporting them. The fate of the four young wives, smuggled out to India "without leave" in the *Thetis*, which sailed from Gravesend on June 4th, 1845 with a draft which included 13 women and 37 children who had drawn lucky in the ballot, is not known.

To be left alone in India was not an easy business, as Delia Turner discovered, and young Mrs. Gilbert who at 24 was left "to the care and protection" of the wife of her late husband's brigadier. Mrs. Brigadier Brown was certainly indignant when her protégée moved into the bungalow of Lieutenant Patrick Craigie. The resultant marriage was solemnised by no less a person than Bishop Heber. Craigie was not only a good husband, but a wonderful stepfather, taking far more care of his pretty stepchild than her mother ever did. It was to his parents in Scotland that he sent Dolores when the time came for her to return for reasons of health and schooling. It was to Patrick that she wrote tear-spattered letters of home-sickness and it was he who found her a situation in Bath with a gentleman who needed a companion for his young daughter.

The engagement could not be counted a success from her employer's point of view, as Dolores eloped with a Captain James. Returning with him to India, she was much admired by Lord Auckland, the Governor-General, and his authoress sister, Emily Eden. Unexpectedly, Captain James ran off with a brother officer's wife, leaving Dolores high and dry and what was worse, managed to divorce her on the grounds of her subsequent misconduct with a Captain Lennox. Altogether, Dolores gave rise to a lot of gossip, which in no way abated as she pursued her meteoric way through life as Lola Montez. But it was not as the mistress of a king that she was finally remembered in India by an old gardener she had delighted to tease. "She was a *badmash*" (bad man), he said with a grin, "and she used to push me into the water, but she was always kind to me".

Of very different metal was Laurentia Sale, wife of General Sir Robert Sale, who with her daughter and other wives and children made the retreat from Kabul to Jellalabad in the snow of an Afghan winter. Kabul was a popular station with the army families in 1842, in spite of the hazards of North-West Frontier life. Housing was good and it was possible to grow flowers and vegetables in pleasant cantonment gardens, even if these were overlooked by wild mountains bristling with invisible watchful frontiersmen. Cricket, race meetings and theatricals were apt to be interrupted by the spitting

6

crackle of rifle shot or talk about the Russian bear with his snout pointed towards India.

Lady Sale, handsome, formidable and kindly, might be thought to have been a typical general's wife. So no doubt she was and much more besides. Had she been in command of the Army of the Indus, it is at least possible that the muddle-headed tragedy of retreat and captivity would not have occurred. But "the only man in the army", as she was once described, could do nothing to straighten the politico/military tangle except to record it minutely in the journal she was determined to publish when the affair was over. So determined, that she endured the terrible marches, the weeks of captivity, the long rides with fever on her and the loss of everything she possessed except the clothes she wore, with the journal tied round her waist in a bag. Her ally in publication was to have been Captain Sturt, her son-in-law, whose warnings to his superior officers about the dangers of the frontier situation were constantly ignored, so that "he became disgusted and contented himself with zealously performing his duties and making himself generally useful, acting the part of artillery officer as well as engineer". If, as Laurentia says, "poor Sturt's life had been spared", they might have exposed as much scandal over quarrels and incompetence in high places as was unearthed after the Crimea.

On Christmas Eve, 1841, it fell upon Lady Sale to break the news to Lady Macnaghten, wife of the political officer, and Mrs. Trevor, whose husband worked in the same department, that both men had been assassinated. Never is her laconic avoidance of sentimentality better illustrated than in her description of this sad task. "Over such scenes", she writes, "I draw a veil. It was a most painful meeting to us all".

She seems to have had a special affinity with her son-in-law and they were wounded on the same day. "Poor Sturt was laid on the side of a bank with his wife and myself beside him. It began snowing heavily . . . some coarse blankets were thrown over us. Dr. Bryce examined Sturt's wound, but I saw by the expression of his face there was no hope. He afterwards kindly cut the ball out of my wrist and dressed both my wounds". A rough tent was erected and the ground inside it cleared of snow. Captain Sturt was helped inside and his six-months-pregnant wife and his mother-in-law were carried through snow too deep to walk in to join him.

It was a terrible night, with Sturt in great agony of pain and thirst. "Most grateful did we feel to Mr. Mein for going out constantly to the stream to procure water. We had only a small vessel to fetch it in". The 30 people packed in together counted themselves lucky, as many died that night in the cold outside. In the morning, they set out again towards Jellalabad, the garrison held by General Sale, and where they would find, if not comfort, at least safety. Mrs. Trevor lent Captain Sturt a pony, the rough motion of which "increased his suffering and accelerated his death". After his death, his wife and Lady Sale "had the sorrowful satisfaction of giving Christian burial" to "my poor son".

These entries, along with all the others, were written at the end of the day and put into the bag with the journal. Though her style is brief and spare and she makes light of her own ills, she gives a graphic and sympathetic account of the sufferings of the wives and children on that dreadful march.

The ladies were mostly travelling in *kajavas* (camel panniers) and were mixed up with the baggage and the column in the pass. On one camel in one *kajava* were Mrs. Boyd and her youngest boy, Hugh, and in the other, Mrs. Mainwaring and her infant, scarcely three months old, and Mrs. Anderson's eldest child. This camel was shot. Mrs. Boyd got a horse to ride and her child was put on behind another man who was shortly after unfortunately killed, the child being carried off by the Afghans. Mary Anderson was carried off in the confusion. Meeting with a pony laden with treasure, Mrs. Mainwaring endeavoured to mount and sit on the boxes, but they upset and in the hurry, the pony and treasure were left behind and the unfortunate lady pursued her way on foot. After a time, an Afghan asked if she was wounded and told her to mount behind him—she declined being fearful of treachery—he snatched her shawl off her shoulders and left her to her fate. Mrs. Mainwaring's sufferings were very great, and she deserves much credit for having preserved her child through those dreadful scenes. She not only had to walk a considerable distance with her child in her arms through deep snow, but had also to pick her way over the bodies of the dead and dying, both men and cattle, and constantly had to cross the streams of water wet up to the knees, pushed and shoved about

by men and animals, the enemy keeping up a sharp fire and several
persons being killed close to her. She, however, got safe to camp with
her child, but had no opportunity to change her clothes, and I know
from experience that it was many days ere my wet habit became thawed
and can fully appreciate her discomforts. Mrs. Bourke, little Seymour
Stoker, his mother and Mrs. Cunningham, all soldiers' wives, and a
child of a man of the 13th, have been carried off.

There is no mention of their having been found. Mrs. Deane, the
wife of a sergeant and herself an Afghan, was particularly useful,
and her friends and relatives brought information that was often of
help to the British. It must have been almost a relief when retreating columns of depleted soldiery, women and children were made
captive by the chief Mahomed Akbar Shah as part of his negotiations
for the surrender of Jellalabad. Indeed, "We luxuriated in dressing,
although we had no clothes but those on our backs, but we enjoyed
washing our faces very much, having had but one opportunity of
doing so since before we left Kabul. It was rather a painful process,
as the cold and glare of the sun had three times peeled my face, from
which the skin came off in strips".

They were not ill-treated and there was plenty to eat, not all of it
very palatable. "Eating cakes of dough is a capital recipe to obtain
the heartburn". Cloth was issued, from which they made themselves
clothes. "I must not use the word dress; and making these gave us
occupation, increased by having to work with raw cotton which we
have to twist into thread for ourselves". Dirt and body lice were the
greatest discomforts, but treated with humour as "Infantry", while
fleas were "Light Cavalry". They lived with rumours flying round
them, though Lady Sale did receive word from her husband and was
allowed to write to him. An attractive child, Tootsey Anderson, was
carried off by Afghans, who took her back to Kabul where they tried
to sell her. Fever raged and there were earthquakes, but there was
delicious fruit to be bought or picked in the gardens of the building
where they were housed. The wives and the ladies enjoyed apricots,
plums and cherries. On April 20th, Mrs. Waller "increased the
community", and the entry in the journal for July 24th begins, "At
two pm, Mrs. Sturt presented me with a grand-daughter, another
female captive". Never was a poignant situation so underplayed. A

week later, she was equally unemotional. "What will now be our
fate seems very uncertain, but I still think he will not cut our
throats". He did not, but it was a further two months before their
release was effected and Laurentia was reunited with her gallant
husband who had received his knighthood for the defence of
Jellalabad during her captivity.

"It is impossible to express our feelings at Sale's approach". And
well it might have been. One can picture the mother and her young
widowed daughter riding towards the general, who must many times
have thought never to see them again. Shabby they must have been,
Lady Sale wearing her *poshteen* and the enormous turban for which
she was famous. (A *poshteen* was a sheepskin coat worn with the fur
inside and embroidered all over the outside. The traditional winter
dress of frontiersmen, it was widely adopted by foreigners.) The girl,
whose joy lay buried among the high and cruel hills, rode beside her
mother, her grief allayed in some sort by the baby carried in its
ayah's arms. Happiness had been so long delayed as to be

> actually painful, and accompanied by a choking sensation which could
> not obtain the relief of tears. But tears came at last when the men of the
> 13th pressed forward to welcome us individually. Most of the men had
> a little word of hearty congratulation to offer, each in his own style, on
> the restoration of his colonel's wife and daughter; and then my highly
> wrought feelings found the desired relief.

After recording that they were greeted by a royal salute of 21 guns,
Laurentia Sale brings what must be one of the best-written, as well
as one of the most remarkable, journals ever kept by a woman to a
typically brisk, laconic close. "And now my notes must end", she
says. "Any further journals of mine can only be interesting to those
nearly connected with me".

Fanny Duberley also campaigned in India and rode with the 8th
Hussars for eleven and a half months. She and Henry had obviously
suffered in health as a result of the Crimea. He was afflicted with
scurvy and travelled in a *dhooley* (litter) while she remained on
horseback till she fainted from the pain of an agonising abscess on
her buttock, which had to be lanced under chloroform. Her

enthusiasm for India waxed and waned. Action was good; the social life boring. Like Lady Sale, she comments acidly on the administration, in this case of the Rajputana column to which the 8th Hussars were attached in the latter part of the Mutiny. She was thrilled at their reception by the Maharajah of Gwalior, who promised her the medal he was having struck, a small, but tangible consolation for the insult after the Crimea.

Sometimes her letters home were cheerful: "I am seeing things and feeling them—better than morning visiting and worsted work". She described Christmas decorations made from mango leaves and flowers, and extra carrots for the horses in celebration of the Nativity. But the country wore her down in the end, as it wore down so many army wives. She rode to the end of her last campaign on November 20th, 1857. It was a historic campaign, in which a hussar of Captain Duberley's regiment slew the brave, extraordinary, infamous Rani of Jhansi as she led her army. Fanny wrote, "out of this damned country I will get as soon as I can". And she did.

Laurentia and Fanny led lives that were both tougher and stranger than those of the average army wife, but few, if any, were out of range of some sort of hazard. Jullundar in the Punjab was recorded by Sergeant Waterfield as being "often visited by dust and rain storms". On July 22nd, 1849, "Rain and hail fell heavily" and a terrific wind swept away the roofs of bungalows. Furniture was blown about and women and children were "sent rolling over for a considerable way along the plain". The wind lasted about 20 minutes. The injured lay about all over the place and women ran distractedly about looking for their children. Two people, a soldier and a child, were killed. The most devastating and tragic of all these instances was the earthquake in Quetta in 1836 which, in the space of a few minutes, destroyed half the town and killed hundreds of people, including army families. But alongside danger lay the gay social life of the memsahib, civilian and military. Fanny may have rebelled, as did one of Henry Wood's daughters and his granddaughter, who both opted out of morning bridge and incessant tea parties in an effort to get to know the country, superficial though that knowledge could only be. But to most army wives, it was the best time they were ever likely to have. The nostalgic yearning for that

fatuous, tittle-tattle existence made them the bores they so often
became in retirement.

It was probably the gay life that drew Mrs. George Lindsay back
to India against the advice of her relatives and the wishes of one
of her daughters. Her attitude is understandable. Rochester must
have been a dull place after Benares, and living there as the widow
of a judge not at all the same as being that judge's wife. The
ostensible reason for going back was to be with George, the only son
and now an ensign in Cawnpore. Her daughter, Caroline, did not
want to go back. The aunts and uncles were against it, but mamma
was adamant. She insisted that they should all go, even Fanny, whom
everyone agreed should still have been at school. Uncle William
Lindsay and Aunt Lilly were there too. Aunt Lilly was mamma's
sister, which was another reason for wanting to go. So off went Mrs.
George Lindsay and her three young daughters, Alice, Caroline and
Fanny.

Caroline could at least find consolation in writing long letters to
the relatives she was so loth to leave. From Barrackpore, Calcutta,
where they arrived in November 1856, comes the account of the
David Lindsays (cousins, conveniently placed) and their "very nice
house". Not that the visitors spent much of their short stay in it.
There were all sorts of gaieties, including a Ball given for them by
the officers, "the room hung with flowers and the colours of the
regiment; two bands, which played alternately, and supper laid out
in a tent". Bed at 2.30 am up again at 9 o'clock to take the train
for Ramnagar, 130 miles away.

On arrival, they found that their arrangements, made well in
advance, had all gone awry and there were no "palkhi gharés,
Englishified carriages" (writes Caroline) ready for them. Incensed,
mamma swept her brood into the waiting room and wrote a note to
the magistrate. The gentleman hurried down to apologise for being
unable to help them till morning and to invite them all to stay with
his wife and himself till the carriages were ready. The Lindsays
were treated with great kindness. Their hosts turned out of their
own bedroom, putting up extra beds so that the tired family could
have a good night's rest.

At 5 pm next day, they started off again and after a few hours came to a river. "No boats to be got", writes Alice laconically, "they said they were all broken, so we had to get coolies, that is men, to pull us over". It was a precarious crossing. The passengers had to get out and sit on the coach box as the water was so high. The operation took two hours by moonlight and there was a journey of several more hours when they finally reached the opposite bank and settled themselves inside the wet carriage. At 9 pm they came to a *Dak* bungalow, where they breakfasted and slept for four hours. (*Dak* means post. *Dak* bungalows were built every 15 miles or so along the main roads of communication to provide accommodation and a change of horses for travellers.)

The next lap went very well until evening. Then, changing horses, "we got a horse that had never been in harness before and commenced rearing, this went on for some time and then it took to kicking and bolting over from one side of the road to the other, so we got out". No sooner had they achieved the comparative safety of the road than the coachman started off at full gallop. The family rushed after him, shouting to him to stop, which he eventually did, declaring he had not known they had alighted, "which was a great story", remarks Alice. Nothing daunted, they clambered back again, travelling till they came to a bungalow and a much-needed breakfast. On again "very nicely" until another horse bolted and then fell down and upset the *gharry*. Surprisingly, nobody was hurt, and they waited on the roadside till the carriage was righted and the boxes which had rolled all over the road put back. Alice and Fanny were involved in this accident, and also George, mentioned here for the first time, who does not seem to have played the role of protective male during this hazardous journey. Fanny and mamma were in another *gharry*.

Three more rivers to be crossed, eight bullocks dragging each *gharry* through low water and patches of sand. On the morning of November 11th, they arrived at Benares, where "we all tumbled into bed, very glad of a rest after four days unpleasant jolting". Their stay at Raj Ghat, five miles out of the city was disappointing, as the distance was too far to permit of sight-seeing, or to visit the old house where mamma used to live when Papa was alive. Colonel Cotton, "an old friend of mamma's", called to see them and announced his intention of giving a dance for the girls. As they were off again on Saturday morning, it was to take place on the Friday night. It was a "very nice dance" and they all went, except George, who turned awkward "and would not go". Of the ten ladies present, several did not dance, so the Lindsay girls were in great demand and danced on into the Indian dawn.

At 8.30, they were on the road again heading for Mirzapur, where they stayed three days. Tuesday and Wednesday were taken up with races, dinner parties and dances, "so", remarks Alice, "I think we shall have gaiety enough". She for one looked forward to their arrival at Cawnpore. "I shall be very glad to be settled for some time, for moving about and stopping first at one place and then another is not pleasant". Mamma might be enjoying herself, but her daughters were tired and a little homesick. In a letter to a cousin, another Caroline, she expects her to write "and give an account of herself", and asks homely, gossipy questions, "Do you still go to Mrs. Webster's to be tortured?" "How is Uncle James and his temper?" "I hope you had a merry Christmas? I suppose it will be over by the time you get this".

Christmas was indeed over, and though she did not know it, Alice's life was nearly over too. But for now, the gay cold weather season was in full swing: parties and dancing, concerts and evening drives, feathers and finery, and no doubt beaux for Caroline, Fanny and Alice. The hot weather began, and so did the rumours of tumult and insurrection in the native regiments. By the middle of May, Mrs. Lindsay was alarmed for her daughters' safety and wanted to get them away, at any rate as far as Calcutta, while she remained at Cawnpore with George. Her brother-in-law, Willy, would not agree to this and insisted that she must go with the girls and that Lilly must accompany them. But for some reason, the move was not made, and on May 19th, Mrs. Lindsay wrote to her sister, Jane Drage. She felt that so many wild stories would have reached England by now that a clear account of the outbreak at Meerut would be welcome.

So she set out the account with a clarity many a man making a report might envy, adding in the middle of the letter and in brackets,

"I forgot to tell you this was in Meerut". This must have been a relief to Jane, who was no doubt imagining the horrors going on round her sister and the rest of the family in Cawnpore.

But any relief felt cannot have lasted long as the letter went on to recount for over nine pages terrible doings much nearer home. Murders of their friends, Mrs. Chalmers "killed by a butcher", a man seized and roasted alive. The reported death of a young friend, "Mr. Willoughby, who left us a month ago" as he gallantly blew up the magazine at Delhi to prevent it falling into enemy hands, made Mrs. Lindsay realise all too clearly how precarious was their situation. (Zoe Proctor records in her memoirs that Captain Willoughby survived the blowing up of the magazine and was awarded the Victoria Cross, one of the first to receive the decoration.)

"If our three native corps were to rise, which I pray to God to avert, we must all I am afraid perish". Better news of Queen's Troops marching on Cawnpore "gave us a more cheering feeling and we all went to church at half past six in the evening and I think we all felt our minds sustained and comforted and trusted that God, who is a good God, would not quite forsake us". Later on, and with an understandable spirit of vengeance, she hopes many of the mutineers "may meet with the death they deserve". In the midst of anxiety and the discomfort of the increasing heat, she does her best to reassure the family at home: "we are all very well thank God . . . all send love to you all, and I pray and hope to be able to send good news next mail". At the very last, her courage falters, "pray for us my dear Jane, my hand shakes, I am hardly able to write".

On May 31st, they went with the other women and children to live in the barracks, as it was no longer safe for them to remain at home. The move was made at half past two in the morning and "you may imagine we were all rather in a fright", wrote Caroline to Aunt Jane Boase. On arrival in the barracks, "the scene of confusion and fright everybody was in was past description". Some found beds, some slept in the carriages, and all were disturbed by a violent thunderstorm, which did at least help to cool the air. "We were all very glad when day dawned", wrote Caroline. They remained in barracks, tightly packed, ten or eleven to a room, but managed "pretty well"

8. The Lindsay sisters: *a*) Caroline; *b*) Fanny; *c*) Alice. They died at
Cawnpore (*By courtesy of* Mr. A. L. Binney)

with *punkahs* (fans) going and *tatties* (grass curtains) well watered, and their food cooked at home and brought up by servants.

Managing pretty well was a demonstration of quiet courage in the face of ever-present fear: "we are still quite in an uncertain state of mind as to what is to be our fate, we only hope and trust we may be defended from all evil". So Alice tells her aunt how much she regrets not being at home to be of comfort to "poor Aunt Susie" on Uncle James' death. Perhaps Alice felt a little guilty about her remarks as to his bad temper.

> Will you kindly send this letter to any of our relatives you like, as I have not much opportunity and place for writing and it is written under difficulties in the dark . . . I hope next mail I may be able to give a better and more favourable account of our proceedings. In health, we are all very well, with best love to all our friends and relations, believe me my dear Aunt Jane, your affectionate niece Caroline A. Lindsay.

The last news from the Lindsay family was given on a scrap of paper found among the tragic welter of personal belongings, clothes and toys found on the floor of the long, low building which came to be known as the House of the Massacre, and to which the women and children were taken as prisoners by the mutineers. Caroline had written:

> Entered the barracks May 21st
> Cavalry left June 5th
> First shot fired June 6th
> Aunt Lilly died June 17th
> Uncle Willy died June 18th
> Left barracks June 27th
> George died June 27th
> Alice died July 9th
> Mama died July 12th

Caroline and Fanny lived for a further three days. Then, sometime between 4 o'clock on the afternoon of July 15th and 9 am of the 16th, they were slaughtered in the long, low building which

9. "Jessie's Dream", F. Goodall's romantic evocation of the approach of the Campbells to relieve Lucknow

(*By courtesy of* Mappin Art Gallery, Corporation of Sheffield)

became known as the *Bibiaghar*, the "ladies' house". The news that
went back to England from the besieged city was appalling. The
Bibiaghar was not the only scene of massacre, as women and
children were treacherously murdered on boats which had been
given safe conduct across the river. General Sir Hugh Wheeler,
commander of the garrison, was himself killed in the fighting, as was
his young son. This family was in a peculiar position with regard to
the Mutiny, as Lady Wheeler was an Indian.

Further details relating to the Lindsays were sent home in a letter
from Captain Moorsom, the 52nd Regiment, to his sister. The letter
was dated July 16th. Captain Moorsom had known Major Lindsay,
the girls' Uncle Willy.

Now for the sad story which I must tell you in as few words as possible
of the poor Lindsays amidst my heavy work here. I have considered it
a duty which I have not neglected where opportunity offered to gain,
for the sake of those who are relatives of my friends, every scrap of
information that I could possibly collect. They consisted of Major
Lindsay and his wife, Mrs. George Lindsay, her three daughters and
one son. Major Lindsay died from the effects of a cannon ball knocking
down the brickwork upon the bed on which he was lying within the
entrenchments; his wife died the day before from fever (17th June) and
their niece died a victim to cholera. The two remaining sisters and their
mother survived the fire and disease within the works, they were
unharmed by the treacherous fire in the boats and imprisoned with
their sisters in affliction and suffered with them on our approach to the
town. Of the son I have been able to gain no intelligence and can only
conclude that he was shot with his brother officers when they went to
the boats. The only comfort I can hope to give to Mrs. Drage and all
their other friends is that, though they were all most ruffianly and
barbarously killed I believe and most solemnly affirm such to be my
belief that their butchers did not ill-use them while alive, nor protract
their suffering when dying. I was the second man inside the house, so
deeply dyed with their blood, nothing should have induced me to go
in had I not known my friends might have been among the number.
I went through the rooms strewn with Bibles and Prayer books and
other religious works, with torn bonnets and clothing, with shoes, some
of little children certainly not more than three inches long, and amidst
all these fearful stains and pools of innocent English blood. Each room

I entered I peered into expecting to see their bodies, but thank God I
was spared that sight, their butchers threw them into a well which we
have had filled in, and upon which we intend to erect a monument.
In this house I could find no token of the Lindsays, though I searched
and caused everything to be collected; one poor girl, at least girl I
fancy her had a great number of books "libra sacra" marked with her
name Isabella Blair, and of these I have kept one little *Companion to the
Altar* either to render to her mother should I ever come across her or
keep myself as a memorial of a day I shall never forget.

Who was Isabella Blair, and what became of her book? It is
unlikely to have been returned to her mother and certainly not by
the hand of Captain Moorsom who was himself killed at the final
attack on Lucknow. Meanwhile, in the short time left to him he continued his harrowing and patient search for anything belonging to
the Lindsays that could be sent home as some slight comfort to their
relatives. He found three books:

... the first their own family record, which I forward to send to Mrs.
Drage (with some small memoranda of my own inside which will
enable their friends to add this sad tale to their history). Another,
Bateman's sermons with this inscription "To Mrs. Lindsay, with the
Bishop of Calcutta's sincere condolences on the death of her infant".
The third an epitome of *Alison's History of Europe* inscribed "Caroline
Anne Lindsay, a prize from her friends the Miss Bohms Christmas
1850".

Captain Moorsom had hopes of finding more of the Lindsays'
belongings in two boxes known to have been left in the care of the
head babu of Major Lindsay's office. It was known that they had
packed away their plate and valuables but nothing was ever found or
heard of and the poor honest babu was erroneously shot in all good
faith while "endeavouring to save some of the major's property" by
someone who took it for granted that he was an enemy and a thief.
  An officer by the name of Ramsay supplies further facts in a letter
of condolence and advice as to how to apply for pensions for the
orphaned children of Major and Mrs. Lindsay, left behind in
England in the guardianship of their uncle the Reverend William

Drage. Ramsay tells Mr. Drage, with regret that "William left no money, his property in his house was all destroyed". He can give him rather better news in that "the allowance from the Bengal Military Orphans' Fund for the three poor children will be paid to you. The sons get it till 19, the daughter till marriage or death without having to return to India. You should apply to Dr. Mackinnan the agent of the Fund in London." This letter written from the Audit Office in Calcutta expresses the writer's deep shock and sympathy with the relatives of the Lindsays, for as he rightly states "few families have suffered like yours—no less than seven adult members of it swept away".

The aftermath of these tragedies, heartbreaking to already heart-broken relatives, is typified by the continued story of the Lindsays. Legal queries immediately arose over the question of who died first. The tragic pencilled list left by Caroline played an important part in settling the question. But there was still the question of whether Fanny was still alive and whether any of the children had survived "to acquire an interest in the trust moneys mentioned in Mrs. George Lindsay's will", which had itself to be proved valid. Then there was the matter of pay and allowances due to Major William Lindsay for the month of May and the first 18 days of June. This was eventually paid to his relatives by the committee of adjustment, arrears due to military and orphans' fund being deducted at source. Every penny was important to Mrs. Drage, who had undertaken the care of the Lindsay children, William, Charles and Mary, while their mother went with Major Lindsay to India and who had now to assume guardianship for the remainder of their minority. The orphans were entitled till they reached the age of 18 to £60 a year from the Bengal Military Orphans' Fund (the same amount as Henry Wood's grandchildren received from the Army after their father had been killed in the First World War). Fortunately, William was a bright boy and won a scholarship to school.

The fact that the Lindsay letters have been preserved by the family means that these sad mothers and their children contribute to their country's history. But there were many more, so many more who disappeared without trace into the sea of hate and blood that drowned them. The Lindsays' Indian servant was murdered by two

British soldiers, who paid for their act of vengeance, we are told in a letter, by being "transported for life". "Poor unhappy Kate", wrote Mrs. Drage to her sister, Mrs. Boase, in October 1857, "dearly has she paid the penalty of searching for happiness in India".

Captain Forrest was a widower when in 1840 he married the fifteen-year-old girl who played happily as a contemporary with her twelve-year-old stepson until she herself became a mother a year after her marriage, giving birth to a boy on the troopship carrying the family to India. Mrs. Forrest was still in her very early thirties when her eldest daughter, not quite 16 years old, became engaged to Lieutenant Montague Proctor of the 31st Native Infantry in May 1857, stationed, like her father, in Delhi.

When the mutineers arrived in the city, young Mr. Proctor and another officer hurriedly assembled a number of women and children, including Mrs. Forrest and her three daughters, and hurried them towards the Kashmir Gate. It was a dreadful beginning to a dreadful journey, as the party had to pick their way over the bodies of people they knew that had, for some unexplained and bizarre reason, been covered over with pretty ball-dresses looted from neighbouring houses. Miss Forrest was shot through the shoulder, but even before the wound could be attended to, she had to be let down over the parapet on an improvised rope made of the flounces of the ladies' dresses, down a considerable height into the deep ditch below, out of which they all had to scramble up a muddy slope.

They were on their own, terrified and helpless, without food or water, making their way as best they could towards Meerut, not knowing the state of that sacked and pillaged station. Indians were kind to them as they passed through the villages and gave them food, and what was more important in the heat of May, water. During the journey, they unexpectedly and joyfully reunited with Captain Forrest, and one of their greatest benefactors was a *fakir*, who hid them during the hours of daylight in the hollowed-out mound that was his hut and his home. He not only gave them food and drink, saying that it was his religious duty to preserve not destroy life, but he noted that the wound in Miss Forrest's shoulder was mortifying and took the matter in hand. His method was terribly painful, consisting as it did of pouring boiling *ghee* (clarified butter) into the wound, but the girl never uttered a sound during the whole operation.

When they had been walking seven days, they came upon a farm belonging to some Germans, who sheltered them. A note, written in French for greater safety, was sent to the General commanding that besieged town. It was taken by an Indian who undertook to pass through the lines undetected. It is only to be supposed that the General did not read French, as he stated it to be "some nonsense" and threw it away. Two young officers had heard a rumour as to its contents and were given permission to set out and find the party. When located, the women were all in a pitiable condition, their bleeding feet bandaged with strips torn from their own dresses, their heads protected, if only a little, from the burning sun with pieces of skirts and petticoats. The youngest Forrest daughter, a child of eight years, had been so terrified the whole time that she had not uttered one word during the eight days it had taken them to reach comparative safety.

The Polehamptons (see p. 17) had a nice house in the Lucknow cantonments, grew English flowers in their garden, and were waited on by ten servants. Henry wrote regularly home, giving details of their life and snippets of information, such as that poor Mrs. Anderson woke from a doze on her sofa to find a cobra with raised hood regarding her from two feet away. Jumping over the snake, she shouted for the servants, who killed it and Henry was shown the corpse. He and Emmie enjoyed their garden, in which grew strawberries, oranges and pomegranates, "Tell me if any scent remains when the flowers I send come to you. Your violets were quite sweet. Thank you for planting the trees for Emmie and me and our darling. He has been transplanted to another soil". Some grains of wheat were sent to them, brought to England from the field of Waterloo but before they had time to watch them grow, Emily was a widow Of this widowhood, she wrote a most moving letter to her mother-in-law.

I cannot tell you what a strange unearthly peace I had at the time of his death. Through that last day and night of his life up to the moment he died, a marvellous kind of triumphant feeling came over me. I cannot explain it, but I felt I was watching his entrance into the joy of his Lord; and I seemed to feel the joy myself. This feeling continued for days after in a greater or less degree, and only became less radiant as the death-blank in my own life became more apparent.

Henry died in the Residency Hospital not of his wound, from which he might have recovered, but from cholera. Emily also tells of having "the great satisfaction of being able to put up a stone over his grave shortly before I left Lucknow. One of the soldiers procured a slab of marble from one of the king's palaces and this I laid upon a plain brickwork he made for me. He engraved the inscription with a small plain cross at the head".

After the death of Sir Henry Lawrence on the third day of the siege, the command of the Residency garrison fell on Colonel John Inglis of the 32nd Regiment, whose wife, Julia, left a day-by-day account of life in the Residency. Sergeant Waterfield, who knew Colonel Inglis before his marriage, tells us that "a greater reformation never was made in any man than was made in Colonel John by his excellent lady. He had the appellation of 'Scaly Jack' before he went on leave to England, but now he is another being".

Fanny Duberley, in one of her sweeping statements, announced that "people in India naturally become idiotic". But though Fanny herself rode in the battle of Jhansi, in which the famous Rani met her death leading her troops, her name is not among those who rank as heroines of the Mutiny, those women, girls and children who, far from being idiotic, endured so much, so bravely, for so long.

Those already in the Lucknow Residency, to which they had been moved at the outbreak of the trouble, were more fortunate than those whose husbands were stationed in outlying places, such as Sitapur. Mrs. Brydon, whose husband, Doctor Brydon, had ridden into Jellalabad as the sole survivor of the fighting in Kabul in 1841, wrote from the Residency to "my dear Travers", addressing someone who knew the place well. She tells of people getting in from Sitapur "saved by the havildar-major and twenty-five sepoys who

protected the rest of the officers and the ladies and children of the
O.I. Infantry Corps, actually escorting them all the way in to
Lucknow". She tells of the Gowan baby, whose father was one of
the first victims to be shot. The ayah thrust the baby up a chimney
in a desperate attempt to hide it and save its life, but next day, its
crying was heard and it was found and shot. And she tells of poor
Captain Evans "whose wife and children are there and anxiety seems
quite to have unstrung his nerves and he has got into disgrace, which
makes me sorry as it is so unlike what I expect of him".

Dr. Brydon was lucky to have been transferred from cantonments
to the Residency, at least in his own opinion and that of his wife.
"The dear wee ones are wonderfully well notwithstanding knocking
about, heat and all disadvantages. We all try to keep brave hearts and
hope for the best—patiently, cheerfully and with thankfulness".

Colina Brydon made a unique contribution to the defence of the
Residency by sacrificing the harp she had brought with her from
home to mend a breach in a wall. The instrument seems to have
come to little harm, as it travelled back to Scotland with her and
remains a family treasure today.

For Madeleine Jackson, the prospect of a winter in India in company with her brother held no fears though, like Fanny Lindsay, one
might have thought she should still have been at school. She and her
sister Georgina and their brother Mountstewart were not army
children, but Madeleine, the only one who lived to tell their story,
became a soldier's wife so it is valid to include them here. Sir
Mountstewart Jackson had inherited his baronetcy while still a very
young boy and was now serving in the Bengal Civil Service. His
widowed mother, like many another mamma before and since, considered the prospects of advantageous marriages for her two
daughters higher in India than they would be at home and dispatched the girls to housekeep for Mountstewart in his bungalow at
Sitapur, not too far away from their uncle, Coverley Jackson, who as
Chief Commissioner of Oudh was living in Lucknow.

The girls arrived in Calcutta on Georgina's birthday after an
enjoyable voyage of four months and two weeks. Madeleine, who
wrote a full account of the experiences etched deeply on her

memory, does not, unfortunately, tell us anything about the clothes they took with them. It seems not unlikely that 70 pocket handker-chiefs, 30 pairs of drawers (or combinations at choice), 15 petticoats, 60 pairs of stockings, 45 pairs of gloves, 20 dresses, as well as shawls and bonnets and parasols would have been the ideal, even if not fully realised. It was also advisable to take a dozen bottles of aperient pills.

From Calcutta, they went to Agra, where they stayed several months with their uncle, who was the commissioner. A dust storm made the journey to Lucknow unpleasant. "It rushed up like a creature", said Georgina, but Mountstewart met them and took them to the bungalow in Sitapur where he was stationed and which they were to share together. It was a nice house and a happy young household, with a lovely garden in which there was plenty of room for the pets: deer, a gazelle, goats, minah birds and pigeons.

Their neighbours, Mr. and Mrs. Christian, were very kind to them and when the rumours of an outbreak among Indian troops became alarming, Mr. Christian tried to hire elephants to get them all away to safety. He was unsuccessful in this attempt and by June 2nd, it was evident that mutiny had broken out and they took refuge in the Christians' house. The mutineers advanced on the house and they all escaped through a french window, Madeleine clinging to her brother's hand. In the confusion, "we lost Georgie", as they ran across an open plain into the jungle. Georgina was trying to help the Christians' nurse and baby and that was the last they saw of her. They ran on and on, and Madeleine pulled off her muslin skirt which kept getting caught on bushes as they ran. Then she lost her shoes. A friendly Indian gave her a sheet "so that I would move like a native. I remember thinking how lovely the jungle was and said to my brother 'I can't bear to be killed'."

They managed to reach a jungle fort where an Indian was protect-ing Captain and Mrs. Orr. The Orrs had servants, a few household goods and money. Somewhere in their flight, they had gathered up little Sophie Christian. Conditions were not too bad, though news came of a poor woman dying, mad, in the jungle and they were unable to find her. Madeleine remained very aware of her surround-ings, of an eclipse of the sun, which was very beautiful, and of the "whizz" some peacocks made when their mating dance was disturbed. But this period of tranquillity was short-lived and they were handed over to the rebels.

Some of the party were put in irons. "Mrs. Orr and I begged them on our knees not to put them on—uselessly—those horrid irons were soldered round each ankle",—two chains which they tied by a string round their waists—"we tore strips of clothing to wrap round them, but even then they made sore places—all day we went on—at every village, crowds came and looked at us, and we looked at them".

She woke in the night to hear some Indians debating whether it would be better just to take the heads of the captives to Lucknow. She remembered how her brother was never frightened and his strength upheld her, though he himself was suffering from fever and another of the party was off his head with sunstroke.

On the night before they reached Lucknow, they prepared specially and prayerfully for death, which they felt was very close, but on reaching the city, they were taken to a house, not, as they expected, to be killed, but to be once more protected. They found themselves in the cool of quiet rooms with a guard. There was English furniture and food, though Madeleine was in pain from crushed fingers, which had been jammed between a soldier's gun and the wall as they were hustled in. Blood spurted from beneath her finger-nails, and the soldier was very distressed and sorry to have caused the accident.

The women were left alone as the Indians took fright at the news of approaching British relief and took the men off. They were all taken to a smaller room, only seven feet high, and were under fire from the Residency, since the British did not know that any of their countrywomen were prisoners in the house. Little Sophie died and Madeleine heard that Georgina had been killed, cut in half by a sword. They were moved to another house and a small girl, Toni Orr, was smuggled out to contact her uncle in the Residency. The owner of this house was a Muslim, Wazid Ali, whose womenfolk gave them clothes, "olive green satin with broad crimson borders, earrings, armlets, bangles and rings". As Madeleine had no holes in her ears, they hung the jewels round them on threads. They also provided dye stuff with which the ladies could stain their skins.

Wazid Ali was very anxious now—it had been found out that he had carried us off as hostages and troops were coming to kill him and us too, so he had got men and fighting was going on. We heard a rush up our stairs and flew out to see what was happening and there was a great tall Englishman. "We are saved", I called out, and ran back to Mrs. Orr. He came in and another Englishman ran up—they said "Are you Miss Jackson and Mrs. Orr? Come at once." A *palkhi* (litter) was got—a lot of little Ghurkas carried us off—up and down ravines like cats—we were in the English camp, saved.

There was comfort and clothes and food, but poor Madeleine was "more frightened than at any other time for fear we should fall into their hands again". The diary account ends with their arrival at Cawnpore, "where Uncle Coverley was recovering from a broken leg". Poor little Madeleine, she was to sustain yet another blow before reaching home and safety. Her brother Mountstewart, who had welcomed his gay young sisters with such high hope, was killed in Lucknow and was buried where he fell in a grassy space surrounded by the swirling traffic of the Hazrutgunj.

There were many accounts of experiences in the Mutiny written by those who survived and many of them were women. Some accounts, those of Henry and Emily Polehampton, Julia Inglis, Mrs. Case and Mrs. Bartrum among them, were published by London firms. Others, like Madeleine Jackson and the Lindsays, remain in the private hands of their descendants. There are fewer accounts from women in Delhi than other places, though some are known to have been captured. In Meerut, the Mutiny broke with such totally unexpected violence that little personal news of it reached the mourning relatives at home.

Most of the narratives, therefore, tell the story of 1857–1858 as lived in and around Lucknow and Cawnpore, and of these, the most remarkable is *The Siege of Lucknow. A Diary by the Honourable Lady Inglis*, published in 1892 by James R. Osgood, McIlvaine & Co. of 45 Albemarle Street, London. There was more than one edition of this diary. The first was a handsome copy bound in marbled board, with a leather spine decorated in gold and printed on beautiful paper, running to 240 pages. In content it is magnificent. The style follows the unemotional lucidity shown by all those ladies who endured similar privations yet who would have screamed at the sight of a mouse, interposed a hand screen between their complexions and the drawing-room fire, and kept to their beds for several weeks after childbirth.

Where Julia Inglis differs from the rest is that she sets out from the beginning to give a clear, reasoned account not only of her own experiences and those of her friends, but of the whole siege

of which struggle I venture to suggest that a thoroughly clear and accurate account has not been given and for this reason. The siege of Lucknow was divided into three parts—the defence under Sir Henry Lawrence and Brigadier Inglis; the reinforcements by Generals Havelock and Outram; and the relief by Lord Clyde. The two first of these parts have been much mixed up in the public mind so that the services of Inglis, Havelock and Outram are often spoken of as being the same. All honour indeed is due to those noble and brave men who came through innumerable difficulties and dangers to our rescue, but they were not the real defenders of Lucknow, for they did not come until after the place had been invested for 87 days. The force before their arrival numbered only about 1,800, opposed by about 15,000 of the enemy. This little band, with its 800 women and children to protect, with barely fighting men sufficient to man the defences, doubtful if it were possible to hold out until relief came, daily losing men from wounds and sickness and exhausted with incessant toil and insufficient food, maintained a defence described by General Outram as unparalleled in European history. The commander during those eighty-seven days was Brigadier Inglis. A month before the siege commenced, he was colonel of his regiment, H.M. 32nd. He suddenly, on the death of Sir Henry Lawrence on the third day of the siege, found himself in this responsible position with the lives of the whole garrison entrusted to his care. It is of this time that I write, hoping that the simple account of each day's events may give a clear idea of what was done by the garrison under his command.

She was greatly assisted in this formidable task by Colonel Birch, the commissioner at Simla, who was her husband's ADC during the siege and who kept careful notes. She begins by describing the situation of the British, military and civilian, at the time when the

32nd Regiment relieved the 52nd in January 1857. The burra sahib
was Sir Henry Lawrence, the chief commissioner, whose headquarters were the Residency, situated in the city close to the River
Gumti and surrounded by the houses of the officials, offices, post
office, hospital and church. His private residence was some three
miles away, close to the barracks of the European Regiment, whose
officers lived in bungalows scattered about the surrounding country.
There were three native regiments officered by British in their own
cantonments. The Inglis family and the other British families lived
in the pleasant conditions of an Indian cold weather. Lucknow is a
fabulous city. The domes and minarets of its mosques, temples and
palaces rise from the deep green of its famous trees and there is, as
Kipling knew, no city in India

> except Bombay the queen of all—more beautiful in her garish style
> than Lucknow, whether you see her from the bridge over the river, or
> from the top of the Imambara looking down on the gilt umbrellas of
> the Chutter Munzil, and the trees in which the town is bedded. Kings
> have adorned her with fantastic buildings, endowed her with charities,
> crammed her with pensioners, and drenched her with blood. She is
> the centre of all idleness, intrigue and luxury... A fair city—a
> beautiful city.

There was no king in Lucknow in 1857. He had been deposed at
the annexation of Oudh by the British. This annexation was considered by some, including John Inglis, to have been a terrible mistake and was one of the causes of the Mutiny. Julia writes of
rumours of the mutinous spirit spreading among the native troops,
though as late as April, they were not considered serious. They were
said to originate in a report spread amongst the sepoys that the
cartridges they were to use for the new Enfield rifle were greased
with pigs' fat with which their mouths would be polluted. A pretext
for revolt was wanted and they used this; the cause was far deeper-
seated.

On May 16th, with news of the horrors at Meerut and at Delhi
in the hands of the mutineers, all the women and children of the
32nd were ordered into the city residency and the ladies were
invited to be the guests of Sir Henry. The move was made at

daybreak. "Hardly a sound broke the stillness of the hour, for no bugles or drums were allowed to sound in order that the time of march might not be known; and a sort of awe came over us, giving us presentiments of evil to come". There was a delay while she waited, mounted and ready to go, with her three children and her friend, Mrs. Case, who had her sister, Miss Dickson, with her. Colonel Case came to fetch them, explaining there had been a delay in the march of the regiment, and they rode off, the three little boys "close to us in carriages. The city was perfectly quiet as we rode through, indeed all the inhabitants seemed asleep".

In fact, the alarm that had caused their evacuation had been a false one and now subsided, though they did not return to their own homes in case of further trouble. They found themselves rather cramped in Sir Henry's bungalow, large though it was. Their visit must have seemed something of an invasion to the grave silent man. He told Julia as she sat next to him at dinner "that he considered the annexation of Oudh the most unrighteous act that was ever committed". The wives and families must have felt almost claustrophobic in the *tykhana* below the Residency building. A *tykhana* was a kind of superior cellar to which people could repair if the heat above ground became intolerable. It was certainly cooler, but there was not much light and the flow of fresh air was fairly inadequate. A fire broke out in the artillery lines which put them in danger, as the wind was blowing in the direction of the Commissioner's bungalow. But it died down and Sir Henry came to tell them "all was right".

May 25th, a Sunday, was the last quiet day any of them were to have. Shots were fired very close to the church, where the ladies were attending evensong, but these proved to be part of the celebrations of the ending of the month-long Muslim fast of Ramadan, and the congregation remained quiet while "Mr. Polehampton preached a beautiful sermon". Next day, with mutiny now hourly expected, all the ladies and their families were sent to the Residency. Julia was distressed on her arrival to find that she was to be parted from her friend, Mrs. Case, and that she was to lodge as one of eight adults and five children in another house. However, in the evening, she went over to the Residency where Mrs. Case was lodged and walked on the roof with her. Below them, "the place was filled with women and children; all seemed very crowded and uncomfortable". It must have been even more so for the women and children in the *tykhanas*. Presumably they were allowed up for air and exercise, but it would have been, regrettably, unthinkable for them to have been allotted quarters in any of the houses in the Residency compound. This was the accepted right of the officers and their ladies. The ladies visited occasionally to assure themselves, to use a favourite expression of Julia's, "all was right" and were presumably satisfied that it was. That there was quarrelling among the soldiers and their families is demonstrated by the shooting by a sergeant major of riding master Eldridge during an argument. Julia says that Eldridge freely forgave his murderer before he died and that both were "steady, respectable men, with large families and liked by their officers". Another source, however, contends that the quarrel was fostered by the wives. The sergeant major was "put in confinement and his poor wife nearly distracted—he was released during the siege and afterwards killed".

The days passed in growing trouble and danger. Julia had to break the news to Mrs. Eldridge of her husband's murder; the news from Cawnpore was bad and getting worse and Julia herself began to feel ill. From the stores they were all beginning to hoard, they sent "some little comforts", tea etc. to a Mrs. Dorin, who had escaped from Sitapur after seeing her husband killed, and had been hiding in the jungle. Julia remained in bed, weaker and more ill with what was found to be smallpox. "Not pleasant news at such a time especially", she recalled, "I was most anxious to be moved to prevent the infection spreading, but this was considered unsafe from shelling, so I reluctantly remained where I was".

The news from Cawnpore was devastating, the whole garrison betrayed and murdered in spite of a treaty with the Nana. It must be stated more than a century after these fearful events that, though they undoubtedly took place in all their bestial horror and the Nana can still be held responsible for failing to stop them, it is now thought not unlikely that this was due to his inability to control a crisis which had mounted to hysterical proportions. His friendship with the British, considered afterwards as deceitful, may have been genuine even though tinged with resentment for a people who, in his opinion, had treated him unjustly.

Julia's fever ran its course, with all the discomfort of high temperature and nightmares. On May 30th, a force left the Residency and later, news arrived that it had been beaten back and was retreating. Ill as she was, Julia got to the window and saw them struggling back, many wounded, all exhausted. But her John, thank God, was safe, though when he came into the room and kissed her, she saw that he was crying. Then he turned to Mrs. Case. "Poor Case" was all he could say. Emily Polehampton took the poor widow who cried out in anguish and dissolved into bitter weeping, away to another room. Soon after this, they were obliged to abandon the upper storey of the house, which had become unsafe as a result of the constant shelling of the building, and take refuge in a small underground room "where the artillery women were quartered". Their butler brought them food and John Inglis managed to get in from time to time to reassure his wife. It cannot have been consoling for the artillery women to have a smallpox patient barricaded in with them, and Julia, although obviously a kindly woman, did not appear to give their possible anxiety a second thought. One of her servants had advised her not to give her jewels into the charge either of the butler or himself as "he evidently thought the temptation of possessing money at such a time might prove too great and might induce them to desert us. And I followed his advice". Servants and their loyalty are frequently mentioned in this diary. Relief came in the evening, when Julia was carried on a sofa to a small room in a neighbouring courtyard and "we all slept, fairly worn out with wretchedness". She was once more sharing a room with Mrs. Case, which was a great comfort to both of them.

Food and clothing grew more difficult as the siege went on and "our ladies were put to sore straits, as they had no servants and had to wash their own clothes. Firewood was scarce owing to the principal stock being turned into a rampart". Ladies risked their very lives to pick up a few sticks, and the palings of the Residency gardens quickly disappeared in this way. At the beginning, every man received a pound of meat and a pound of flour per day; this was reduced first to 12 ounces, then six, and after the arrival of Have lock's force, to four ounces. Women got threequarter rations, children half, and there was no bread, butter, milk, eggs, vegetables, wines, beer or tobacco. There was much sickness and a great mortality among the children.

Trevelyan, writing his history of the Mutiny at Cawnpore, states with truth that "it is impossible for an Englishman to realise the true character of the great troubles unless he constantly bears in mind that all was done beneath the vertical rays of an Eastern summer and in a temperature varying from a hundred and twenty to a hundred and thirty-eight degrees".

Compared to those in Cawnpore, the families in the Residency were safe and almost comfortable, which is saying little enough. At least they did not have to witness the corpses of an English lady and gentleman—floating down the river from some distant scene of death—that had been turned aside into the canal that traversed the city. Though wires had been cut, mails burnt and every road blockaded, those silent but unimpeachable messengers in virtue of the safe conduct granted to them alone were long destined to carry from station to station the tidings of woe and dismay.

It is left to a splendid woman, Bridget Widdowson, to supply the one bit of comic relief that ever came out of Cawnpore. She was a great strong woman, wife of a private in the 32nd Regiment, and was standing around when eleven mutineers were captured and brought into the entrenchment which was the sole British defence. No sentry was available to guard them, so they were handed over, roped insecurely together wrist to wrist, to Mrs. Widdowson. She sat them on the ground like good schoolchildren in a row while she marched up and down in front of them, a drawn sword in her hand. "After she had been relieved by a warder of another sex", says Trevelyan, "they all managed to slip off".

In Lucknow, the siege dragged on. Julia fretted at being unable to help nurse the sick, but was comforted by the fact that her husband managed to dine with them most evenings, and that they had time to read the day's psalms and pray together before he left her for the long dangerous day ahead. Her ayah's husband and children were outside, which made the poor woman very miserable, but her loyalty to the family never wavered. Horse fodder ran shorter and shorter and good animals had to be turned out of the Residency. Julia was anxious about her youngest child, who was ailing, but she managed to get some toys from a merchant outside as presents for her eldest, Johnny, on his fourth birthday. A further worry was the illness of Mrs. Case, diagnosed by the doctor as "suppressed grief".

At last the siege came to an end, and the women and children left the Residency on November 17th, 1858. Their first night away from the place that had been their enforced home for so many weary months was spent in even stranger, more macabre surroundings. The *Secundra Bagh* was a beautiful house standing in a large garden, and here, only a few days earlier, terrible retribution had fallen on the rebels. News reached the army of the massacres at Cawnpore and the men instantly slaughtered every Indian within range, the total number of dead being in the region of 1200. The bodies were "just covered over with earth", Julia tells us, "and it sickened me to feel they were so near us".

Life began to be rather easier, "I hope I was not very greedy", says Julia, after having been asked to breakfast by the officers of the 9th Lancers, "but I certainly appreciated the good things with which their table was loaded". She went to see the women of the 32nd "who had a tent to themselves and looked so happy and comfortable". On December 6th they reached Allahabad, after a journey which had taken them through Cawnpore. "The residents of Allahabad were indeed most kind in the way they received us and thankful did we feel once more to be in a place of security and rest". The place allotted to them was a grassy walled space within the fort and there they lived in tents till the steamer came to take them down river to Calcutta. The first steamer took off the widows and sick ladies, among them Mrs. Case, and her going was a sad loss to Julia, as they had remained close friends through so much tribulation. On Christmas Day, Julia gave a dinner for the women and families of the 32nd. "It was anything but a festive sight to me. Nearly all were widows and every child present had lost one or more parents". During the time they were all in Allahabad, Emily and Mrs. Harris had established a school for the children, and Julia had the children of the 32nd on Sundays.

The journey homewards continued in slow stages and they had one more severe trial to undergo. Julia said good-bye to the remaining women and children of the 32nd and sailed on February 10th from Calcutta, pleased to be once more in the company of Mrs. Case and her sister. They enjoyed a few pleasant hours on shore at Madras and then proceeded towards Trincomalee in Ceylon, where they had to put in briefly to land treasure. But on the night of February 10th they struck a rock and the women and children were ordered into the lifeboats. Julia, Mrs. Case and her sister "communicated our determination to keep together under all circumstances".

The party in their boat consisted of "Mrs. Bruere, four children and nurse; Mrs. Cowie and one child; Mrs. Case; Miss Dickson; Mrs. Campbell, my nurse, and her daughter; myself and three children—one of the officers commanded the boat and steered". Distress signals were sent up, but were not observed, and the boats were rowed backwards and forwards all night between the rocks to prevent their being wrecked. A tribute can here be paid to Mrs. Bruere's Irish nurse, who kept them all laughing by her absurd remarks. "She was quite a character in her way", says Julia. "Day at last broke", she goes on, "and threw light on a curious scene—our seven little boats tossing up and down crowded with passengers; for the sea which had been calm was now rather high, rocks and breakers on all sides". The captain, who remained aboard, issued orders for the boats to make for Trincomalee, ten miles away, and to send back assistance.

On getting clear of the reef, we found the sea very rough and the wind against us; our boatmen, who were wet through, were very tired and our boat, a very bad one leaking fast—we had some wine which we mixed with water and gave to the men, but they were very despondent and seemed to have lost all heart; myself baled for a little while just to encourage them and this, giving me something to do, cheered me up. The waves were very high and each one looked as if it would swamp us. Johnny was delighted when they broke over the boat and his merry laugh sounded sadly in my ears, for I quite thought a watery grave awaited each one of us.

When a sail was sighted a long way off, signals were made, but the ship seemed to be going in the opposite direction. Their relief at the realisation that the vessel was, in fact, approaching them was tempered by instructions to conceal any ornaments or money before being taken aboard.

> This was anything but agreeable . . . (to Julia or any of the others, as it was evident the boat might be a pirate one). With great difficulty, we were hoisted on board. The nurse, an immense woman, hung for some time midway and I really thought the men would drop her. As soon as we were on board, the crew told us we must go below. We refused, thinking it was a trap for us, but they said they could not navigate the ship if we remained where we were. We consented, therefore, to be lowered down the hatchway, another difficult operation. We certainly judged the poor men wrongly, for they were most kind to us, spread sails for us to sit on, made curry for us to eat and gave us hard boiled eggs. The children ate ravenously, having had nothing but a few crumbs of biscuit since the evening before. For my part, (says poor Julia, using a very Victorian expression), I was too done up to eat.

They reached Trincomalee and safety, and Julia, Mrs. Case and Caroline Dickson went still together to one house. Every house in the British cantonment was opened to help the refugees and "the soldiers gave up their tea the first night so that we might have bread enough, as being a small town, there was no superfluity of provisions". A small, uncomfortable steamer took them to Suez, and in cramped and crowded conditions, the women set about making makeshift clothes for themselves and their children, having lost everything but what they were actually wearing in the wreck. At Suez, reached after two fire alarms on board, life suddenly assumed an aspect of normality for Julia, who heard that her father had been made Lord Chancellor. With only one more lap to go, the three friends parted at Alexandria.

> We had lived together since our trouble commenced on the most intimate terms—I owe them much gratitude for their unvarying kindness to me and my children; the cheerfulness with which they submitted to innumerable inconveniences and annoyances; and above all, the noble example they set me of unselfishness, Christian fortitude and resignation.

Writing her account 30 years later, she pays a final tribute to the two who, in spite of their mutual intimacy, she never refers to by anything except their married names and titles. "They are, and ever will be", she says, "two of my best and truest friends". Then came Southampton and home and the loving welcome of her family. "The past seemed forgotten; and if only John had been with me, my cup would indeed have been filled to the brim". Sir John joined her some months later. The Inglises remain remarkable, not only for what they were, but as one of the few couples who both lived to tell their story.

Emily Polehampton's last act before leaving the Residency was to visit the churchyard. "What would I not give to be resting there with him. God only knows how I have longed to die and there to be buried". On hearing that they must prepare to leave, "I burnt all my papers, clothing and letters, in fact all I had in the world save a few things I kept in our overland box on the chance of bringing it away. All my husband's sermons I cared about most I wore in a large pocket round my waist; his gown, surplice hood and stole and baby's clothes I sewed into a pillow".

At the last minute, preparations, orders and counter-orders were given and rescinded. Emily discovered too late that she could have saved all her belongings, as each lady was to have a camel for her own use. She had not, fortunately, destroyed the harmonium which had been presented to her by the men of the 32nd Regiment. Unlike Mrs. Brydon's harp, it had lain idle and unharmed during the siege and this was now loaded onto the camel and eventually arrived safely in England. Throughout the journey home, her concern is always for the sick and wounded, be they men or women.

Before they reached Cawnpore, the heat had become very great and she was particularly worried about a poor girl, half of whose hand had been shot off by the accidental firing of a gun which was lying loaded in the cart in which she travelled. No *dhooley* could be procured for her and she was obliged to march, since, expecting her confinement within a month and in the pain and shock she was in, the shaking of a bullock cart "would almost certainly have been fatal". Emily, herself not four years older than the 21-year-old widow, noted "the black leaden look" about her face with apprehension.

A gift box arrived from Lady Canning for distribution among the "Lucknow ladies" when she reached Allahabad, and Emily and Mrs. Harris distributed them. "Shoes, boots, brushes, stockings, handkerchiefs and soap etc.", notes Emily with pleasure. She took her turn at school teaching, but her mind was always taken up with the wounded, visiting them in the hospital tents, trying to secure a place on the first steamer and be allowed to nurse.

Among the sad souvenirs packed in her luggage, she now added relics found lying about in the chapel at Cawnpore, the ruined home of many of the women and children during the siege. She and Mrs. Barbor picked up pieces of music and torn drawing paper, but did not, fortunately, see anything so terrible as the long, beautiful plait of hair torn out by the roots found by an officer. Emily had not been able to attend church for many months, as the building had had to be converted into a grain store during the siege and in any case it would have been far too dangerous. Unlike Julia Inglis, who had the consolation of reading the services very often with her husband, Emily had been spiritually lonely except for her own unwavering faith. December 13th was a Sunday and Mr. Harris held a thanksgiving service with Holy Communion for the survivors of the Lucknow Garrison in the fort chapel. Poor Emily!

It was the first time I had been at a service of any sort since May 24th when I was with my own dear husband—the sight of the Communion table and everything as in old times was almost more than I could bear. What would not this service have been to me if *he* had been there to celebrate it. I have always such a *craving* for his presence at these times of service; and yet well I know how selfish this is.

Physical and emotional craving burns bright in these last words, unusually frankly expressed for one of her day. She was also very much worried over the unsuccessful attempts to trace the Jackson sisters—"those poor girls. They were so pretty and so fond of each other", and for the effect it was all having on their uncle, under whose chaperonage they had come to India.

INDIA 115

At every stopping place on this journey towards home, the women
and children were objects of curiosity and homage which, though
understandable, was tiring for those who received it. By the time
they reached Calcutta, Emily and the young widowed Mrs. Bartrum
who was travelling with her preferred to lodge in one of the "Houses
of Refuge" provided by the Relief Fund than accept the liberal
offers of hospitality offered them. Their decision was strengthened
by the illness of Mrs. Bartrum's little boy, which grew daily worse
until the dawn hour when the mother called Emily to her room
"terrified by the change in him, scarcely knowing what it was. I,
however, knew only too well. But she was very very good, and I
persuaded her to keep quite quiet, so as not to disturb the dear little
child in his last moments, and he died in her arms". Then Emmie
did for her friend's child what she had been too ill to do for her own,
after which "we gathered roses and other flowers from the garden to
lay around him." The next day, Emily and Mrs. Bartrum boarded
the *Himalaya*. Friends saw them off, providing additional comforts
in the shape of an armchair and a print of "Hagar and the Angel"
for Emily's cabin, while she had the satisfaction of knowing the
harmonium was safely stowed away in the hold. After a long, but
comfortable, voyage, they landed at Plymouth on June 8th, 1858,
and a paragraph added to her journal by one of her brothers-in-law
tells us that "she proved indeed a ministering angel to the poor
wounded fellows whose sufferings and deathbeds she comforted and
relieved".

The Great Indian Mutiny was over. Probably nobody will ever be
able to make a fair assessment of the rights and wrongs of both sides,
the seething resentment that was its cause, the fear it engendered
among the British, particularly the women, a fear that neither the
government nor the army took any steps to allay. Nearly a century
later: "It is unfortunate", said Kunwar Sahib Jasbir Singh of
Lucknow to Henry Wood's granddaughter, "that Englishwomen
since 1858 have always thought that every Indian has a knife in his
hand".

There would certainly have been no thought of wars or mutinies on
March 1st, 1866, when Major Henry Wood, Rifle Brigade, married

nineteen-year-old Frances, daughter of Major General Smith in Rawal Pindi. Ten years had broadened Henry from the slim ensign of the Crimea to a handsome brown-bearded man. Somewhere along the line in that decade, he had developed his passion for photography into a highly individual style and his cumbersome equipment went with them on their honeymoon. The honeymoon itself was unconventional, which might have surprised Frances, but nobody else who knew Henry then or later. Casting off the crinolines which showed her tiny waist off to such advantage, she donned thick boots, short skirt and a *poshteen* and slogged beside Henry up mountain paths, over rickety bridges and on to glaciers. Wrapped in a shawl against the mountain cold, she drank tea outside their tent under the pines, or, the climbing over, leaned against the cushions of a boat in Kashmir, fragile and feminine again, her smooth head bent over the bell rope she was embroidering in Berlin wools. Twelve years her senior, Henry clearly found his bride ravishing and posed her again and again among ruined temples, in her storeroom surrounded by jars and weighing scales, on horseback, and composing at her square piano in their bungalow at Pindi. But Frances died of scarlet fever after they had returned to England, and Henry was left with two fragile little children and memories of three short years of happiness.

It could be said that the army wife had now entered her heyday in India. Spectres of sickness and of leaving the children behind in England still stalked, but they could be kept at bay by an incessant round of dinner, shooting and garden parties; polo; theatricals; leave spent in Kashmir; the romance of the Taj Mahal by moonlight and the double gaiety of two "seasons"—hot weather in the hills, cold weather on the plain. Certainly, the memories and terrors of the Mutiny still lingered, but women were now very secure in cantonments and the military was self-supporting, with contractors to supply its every need and no cause to go near a bazaar to shop or have anything to do with a single Indian, except the servants. The ruined bungalows had been rebuilt, the scorched gardens bloomed again and children played in safety amongst the flowers. Life for the Raj had speeded up. Mails were quicker and parcels could be sent from shops at home if you could not find what you wanted in the stores opening in Calcutta and Bombay. The *dhurzee* (tailor) could copy almost anything from a fashion plate and every army wife had one sitting on her verandah for days at a time, cross-legged in front of his sewing machine, or shifting about on his haunches as he measured and cut, using his toes as extra fingers to hold the cloth. Cantonment life was parochial, flirtatious and gossipy.

Sometimes, the gossip flared into malice, as it did in Mhow in 1861, when an extraordinary build-up of chit-chat and acrimony resulted in the divorce case in which an officer's wife had featured causing the death of a sergeant in the 6th Inniskilling Dragoons. Captain and Mrs. Renshaw were a popular couple and happily married. Then the word got round that Mrs. Renshaw had been the guilty party in a divorce case. The man who unearthed this care-fully-hidden secret was the regimental paymaster Captain Smales, who, since divorce was not countenanced in the army, and from the security of his own impeccable marriage to the daughter of a colonial governor, demanded the social ostracism of the Renshaws by the regiment, the 6th Inniskilling Dragoons. Colonel Crawley, the new commanding officer just arrived from England, found himself in the middle of a seething situation of mounting acrimony which he was entirely unable to control and which, like a dust devil sweeping across a desert, drew several unlikely people into its centre.

One of these people was Regimental Sergeant Major John Lilley, another his wife Clarissa. It seems incredible that a purely social scandal relating to an officer and his wife should have resulted in the arrest of the RSM for insubordination, but this was India and the hot weather at that, and by the time of Lilley's arrest everything had got completely out of hand. The RSM was a big burly man of 37 who liked a glass of beer. His wife Clarissa was 15 years younger, consumptive and grieving for their two children who had both died only two weeks before Lilley's arrest. Clarissa's condition was so bad that she was due for admittance to hospital but she declined to go, begging to be allowed to remain with her husband for the short time left to her and the couple were allowed to be together on com-passionate grounds, existing in a small badly ventilated room under heavy guard pending Lilley's court-martial. But before this took place, Lilley died of heat stroke and it was left to Clarissa to write the letter home that broke the news.

My dear sister and brother, this is indeed a painful moment, a task I never expected to have to tell you. My beloved husband is no more. Dear sister go in mercy to our father and mother, I cannot write to them, the blow will be too much. I am staying with Sergeant Major and Mrs. Cotton. I was to have gone to hospital, but doctor says I shall not last long, so I don't think I shall be removed before anything happens. I cannot write any more, I cannot sit up. My best love, your loving and affectionate sister, Clarissa Lilley.

She died next day. The army took this and other scandals in its stride; Indians stood by and kept their own counsel; life went on.

References to Chapter 5

Annals of the Indian Rebellion, N. A. Chick, ed. D. Hutchinson, Charles Knight, 1974
Cawnpore, G. Trevelyan, Macmillan, 1886
Company I Have Kept, H. S. Salt, Allen & Unwin, 1931
The History of Afghanistan, 3 vols., J. W. Kaye, 1857
Last Post at Mhow, A. Hawkey, Jarrolds, 1969
Life and Yesterday, Z. Proctor, Favil Press
The Siege of Lucknow, Lady Inglis, Osgood McIlvaine, 1892
The Siege of Lucknow by a Staff Officer
A Traveller's Handbook, E. Roberts, 1837

The Chronicle of Private Metcalfe, Metcalfe, Cassell, 1953
The Diary of Madeleine Jackson, India Office Library
The Diary of Mrs. Bartrum, India Office Library
The Diary of Mrs. Case, India Office Library
Diary of Mrs. Sherwood, Mrs. Sherwood, Houlston
A Journal of the Disasters in Afghanistan 1841–42, Lady Sale, John Murray
A Memoir, Letters and Diary of the Rev. Henry Polehampton, Richard Bentley, 1858
Sergeant Pearman's Memoirs, ed. The Marquess of Anglesey, Cape, 1968

6. *Living Abroad*

GOING ABROAD DID not always mean going to war. Military families led agreeable lives for several years at a time in India, China, Bermuda, Mauritius, Ceylon and elsewhere. Charlotte McCarthy, daughter of the Governor of Mauritius, married Colonel Robert Owen of the 72nd Highlanders in 1814 and the couple remained on the island for two years after their marriage. She recorded the daily happenings of her life in a small home-made diary, its folded sheets of hand-made paper stitched together with white sewing thread. The outside sheets used as covers are used for notes and rough calculations:

$$\begin{array}{r} 39 \\ 24 \\ \hline 63 \\ \hline \end{array}$$

written twice as though she did not altogether trust her powers of addition. Follows the note July 15th, 17 bottles of beer; 26th ditto empty, while from entries on the back, we learn that she paid:

Mama	£1.00.1½
Ranchard	£1.00.0
Nurse	£2.14.3

Ranchard was her doctor and there is another slightly mysterious entry regarding him: "Took Carla from Ranchard". At first sight, this might be supposed to be a little daughter who had perhaps been ill and cared for in his house, but Charlotte, married at 20, did not have a child till she was 32. The Owens started their married life in a house called "Mon Plaisir", from which Charlotte constantly "drove to town", though not quite as often as she wished, judging from two wistful entries recording the fact that the French Bachelors had given a ball and the Military another, both at the Petit Cercle, and to each of which they "did not go". Papa's office caught fire one night and was completely consumed, except for the public chests.

Mamma and Charles got out, but all might have been saved if they could have procured water. Sir A. Campbell gave her "a ridicule", but there is nothing to indicate if this is a way of saying that he teased her, or if he made her a present of the kind of purse known as a reticule and that her spelling was shaky. Lady Campbell also gave her a present of a pearl hoop ring. She was very health-conscious on her own account and Robert's. Having been taking her drops regularly at the rate of ten drops a dose, she increased them to 20, while Robert began taking his Cheltenham Salts. She wrote frequently to England for muslin, sarcenet and ribbons and to Mamma, who had sailed with Papa to the Cape. Robert wrote to Sophie.

The Owens left "Mon Plaisir" and went to live at Powder Mills, where they gave a dance, which was perhaps the reason for having the piano tuned. "Robert began wearing his socks" and one and a half dozen pairs were sent to Mamma, presumably to be worn by Papa at the Cape. Robert also began wearing his shirts, and a mango grown at Black Rover and sent to Sir A. Campbell weighed two pounds ten and a half ounces. "Poor Mr. and Mrs. Hill had a sad time of it. First of all, a fire broke out behind their house and spread. Furniture and public papers were saved, but Mrs. H. lost all her jewels". Not long after this they were both thrown out of their gig while on an evening drive and Mr. H. died of a contusion on the back of the head.

For two days after setting sail for England in 1816, Charlotte was very sea-sick, but recovered sufficiently to walk on deck on the third day, after which it was calm. It seems to have been an enjoyable voyage and they left their frigate one evening to dine on board the *Horatia* and watch a play performed by the sailors.

It is a tantalising little book because of what lies unstated behind the brief entries. Who was Mary, whose address was c/o Couttenden and McKillop, Calcutta? Does anyone now remember her? Did Charlotte send many garments to be dyed by Mr. McGill of Windmill Street, London? How many of them went by waggon to the races in Cape Town and why the single mysterious entry "Trade Winds"? But it is on St. Helena, with its illustrious prisoner, that Charlotte excels herself in understatement. Her entry during the visit reads simply, "anchored at eight o'clock. Went to Plantation

House in Sir Hudson Lowe's carriage, drawn by four bullocks".

Juana Smith made the long journey to South Africa with her husband, who as General Sir Harry Smith was Governor of Cape Colony from 1847–1852, and named the town of Ladysmith after his Juanita. Any talk of war she heard now concerned Boers and Kaffirs. Nor can the wide stretches of empty country under the wonderful African light have reminded her of the difficult country she rode over as a girl with fighting all round her, nor Table Mountain and the Hottentot Hollands recall the mountains of her native Spain.

The Reverend Mr. Buckner, an officer in the Rifle Brigade before taking holy orders, was posted to South Africa in 1849 as the first chaplain to go there. Travelling in comfort and alone, he preceded his wife by two months, leaving her to bring out eight children, with another on the way. The mother was brought to bed of a son two months prematurely immediately on her arrival, "no doubt", as his granddaughter remarked, "from the sheer relief that the voyage was over".

Colonel John Briggs began his career by running away to join the army in 1846, at the age of sixteen. As they had destined him for the church, his angry parents bought him out, but he escaped a second time and enlisted in the 9th Regiment of Foot, rising quickly from corporal to sergeant. By 1850, he had become orderly to the Duke of Cambridge, and had married. When the time came for his posting to Malta, Margaret Briggs drew lucky in the ballot, so was able to take her two young children with her. The Briggs party was completed rather oddly, but most fortunately as it turned out, by the sergeant's sister. They lived very comfortably in St. Elmo until seven months later when Briggs, then colour sergeant, embarked for the Crimea. Margaret and their son succumbed to Malta fever and the aunt took care of the little girl till the father came from the Crimea to take them home.

Some wives went with their husbands on special postings. An

appointment as military attaché in a foreign country was popular and there were various secondments to which the soldier was permitted to take his wife. One of Henry Wood's granddaughters will always remember with longing the wild splendour of Kurdistan, the fierce beauty of its people, its legends and feuding and fighting. Colonel Henry Wood took his second wife and their children to India in 1878 —a typical army family. Husband and wife, three little girls, a nice bungalow, servants, ponies, pets and picnics. Helen Wood differed widely in type from her predecessor. She had dark hair swept back from a rather stern, handsome face, and her tall, willowy figure was so graceful that even her young grandchildren were aware of its beauty in her old age. Her character matched her appearance. Upright, controlled and at least outwardly composed, she endured many years of an unhappy marriage, doing her duty in the state of life into which it had pleased the God she firmly believed in to have called her.

There was never any gossip about Mrs. Wood. Her admirers, of whom there were more than one, offered their attentions with respect, while Henry went his own photographic way. His photographs, highly regarded today, brought groans from his daughters for the rest of their lives. "Papa's camera—how we loathed it—we were always being made to pose for him". Like Frances, Helen looked wonderful on a horse and rode beautifully. At the Simla Horse Show, she won a silver cup for jumping her horses, Skylark and Jackal.

The extraordinary thing about army life in India was that it remained entirely unchanged for three generations. Hazel Close and Olive Grissell, Henry's daughters, returned to the conditions of their childhood—nice bungalows, servants, ponies, pets and picnics; oil lamps and frilly drawing-rooms. Day after day went by in enjoyable monotony, often beginning very early in the morning with a ride round the perimeter of the station, but never venturing farther afield because that would mean going into villages where Indians lived. Back at home, the *syce* (groom) would be waiting at the stables to take the horses, tendering pieces of *jagri*, the unrefined English sugar bought in cones and used by the British only in the stables The *syce*'s family, who lived in much the same conditions as the

10. "Posing for Papa" in this picture are Helen Wood and her daughter Olive, the grandmother and mother of Veronica Bamfield. For all its simple appearance this is a fake—officers' wives did not do their own cooking.

animals (and good conditions these were), stood about salaaming, and the sahib gave orders for the day as to when the pony trap was to be brought round and when the memsahib and himself would be ready for their evening ride.

Breakfast was taken on the verandah or indoors, according to season, with porridge and eggs and bacon, or the splendid dish beloved of Indian cooks, "Rumble Tumble Andar", a translation of scrambled eggs. It is to be hoped that with the passing of the Raj, the comic Indian versions of traditional British dishes, especially the Rumble Tumble and Irish Eshtew, will remain, since India would be the poorer for their going. The army wife kept a very British table, both in the dining-room and the nursery. With the exception of fruit such as mangoes and papaya, melon and *tipari*, everything was as near to the taste and standards of home as possible. *Tipari* were Cape gooseberries which were served as a dessert, the petals peeled back and the fruit covered in white icing. They looked like some sort of insect and were delicious. The Mrs. Beeton of India was Flora Annie Steel, whose *Complete Indian Housekeeper and Cook* was the culinary Bible of every British home. After its publication by Heinemann about 1887, it ran into ten editions and was translated into the vernacular. It was still in use in 1940. It is dedicated by Mrs. Steel and her co-author Miss Grace Gardiner:

To
The English girls
to whom
Fate may assign the task of being
House mothers
in our eastern Empire

and it told the house mother literally everything she wanted to know, from what she should pay for furniture made to pattern from British catalogues, to a remarkable recipe for home-made cement which, declare the authors, will prove strong enough to hold pieces of pressed steel together. Between these extremes lie instructions for dressing, eating, drinking and home nursing, and hundreds of recipes.

According to Mrs. Steel, all the ordering of the household should be done before breakfast and the memsahib would have her life so organised that half an hour would suffice for this. It is open to question whether many army wives were as dedicated as that. For most of them, the store-room was unlocked after breakfast. The memsahib went in among the sugar (white), the tea, salt, flour, tinned goods, soap, scouring powder, wines and spirits, soda water, polishes, candles and a dozen other things, to dole out precisely what was needed for the day. She ordered the meals, checking the cook's expenditure of the day before and giving him money for current buying. After this, she would inspect the kitchen: a building set apart from the house, its stove a rectangle constructed of dried mud, in the top of which were large holes connected with a draught lower down. These holes were filled with charcoal and the *dechsies* (handle-less saucepans, "dixies") placed on the top of them. The cook's boy fanned the charcoal from beneath to maintain the heat. The oven was a tin contraption placed on top of one or more of the holes.

Terrible stories are told of the goings-on of Indian cooks; socks discovered in a saucepan of soup, fishcakes pressed into shape by squeezing in the armpit and so on. But it is doubtful if they were worse than their kind anywhere else: the good ones were very good indeed and all could have been better had they been allowed to introduce the sahib and his family to the food of their own caste and country. The cook did try to brighten up dull dishes by making them more colourful. Mashed potatoes looked, to his eyes at least, far more attractive disguised as apples, their cheeks rosy with cochineal and a clove for a stalk; but the memsahib frequently forbade him to do this, which was a disappointment.

The household servants of a married officer usually consisted of a bearer; the head servant, the *khitmatghar* (or major domo) who usually had a boy to help him; the *masaclchi*, who looked after lamps, fires and bathwater; a nursery boy, where necessary; and a sweeper, who managed the sanitary arangements which were simple. Every bedroom in the house had its own bathroom, furnished with a tin bath, a washstand and a thunderbox. This was an extremely comfortable commode, with arms and a bucket. When the session was over, the user of the thunderbox opened the bathroom door that led outside and yelled. The bucket was taken away immediately, emptied and returned with creosol solution in the bottom. Another distinctive feature of the bathroom was the Bromo. It is doubtful if in the length and breadth of India, any other lavatory paper could have been found. It came, a certain number of sheets at a time in a black and yellow container, on the front of which was printed a great deal of information about its apparently almost miraculous properties and the warning that those who did not take advantage of these would certainly suffer from what was described as the painful "and almost universal complaint called *piles*". The bath stood on a slightly raised platform, with built-up sides and a draining hole. Hot water was poured in from copper vessels or, later on, empty kerosene tins, and the bather added the cold from a huge Ali Baba jar with a tin dipper. The dirty water was tipped on to the platform by the sweeper and ran outside through a hole in the wall. To lie in water heated over charcoal, or better still, as in the hills, wood, is an experience that bathers in tap water can never know, to their deprivation. It is also an experience much despised by all Indians, including the low-caste sweeper, who washes under running water every day and considers the white man a dirty creature. Another point of difference with regard to sanitation is the disgust felt by Europeans at seeing the Indian in the street blow his nose with his fingers and flick the result on to the ground. "And have you ever thought", asked Kunwar Jasbir Singh, himself educated in England, "that it is even more disgusting to blow your nose on a piece of rag and put it into your pocket?"

At the beginning of this century, a bearer received ten rupees a month, a cook fourteen, a *khitmatghar* ten, a *masalchi* six, the *dhobi* or washerman ten, and a sweeper six rupees per month. The rupee was worth one shilling and sixpence. The household servants all had uniform provided, white for the hot weather and wool for cold, and quilts. They lived in rooms called go-downs, away from the house but part of the compound. There were also the outside servants *syces*, *malis* (gardeners) and their inevitable assistants.

One of the most popular recreations was a trip to Kashmir, and thirty years after Henry and Frances Wood had honeymooned there

11. The drawing room of the Indian bungalow of Henry and Frances Wood. Note the punkah ropes on the ceiling; and in the dining room beyond; the punkah was the Indian system of air conditioning

Captain Ward of the Queen's Bays set off with his wife and their eighteen-month-old daughter for Srinagar. They started from Murree on June 15th on a long leave of three months, during part of which Jeanette Ward had cause to wonder if they had done right in bringing a child so young as little Rosa. Her anxiety was partly due to the difficulty in getting milk. From their houseboat on a lake just outside Srinagar, she and Tom

> saw a large herd of cows grazing, so were determined if possible to get some. No good trusting to servants, so Tom and I went off ourselves with a milk jug and a lot of the servants followed. The sweeper caught a cow and another man milked a few spoonfuls from her, but that was all she had. There was great difficulty in catching another, but the sweeper did so, this time by the tail, but it galloped about with him holding on to its tail and seemed to have no intention of stopping, so he caught it by the tail and brought it down, but alas, it had no milk. The cow-man was then seen in the distance and the *khit* gave him chase, they had a long run but the cow-man was uncaught and we had to retire disappointed onto our boats. I liked to see the cows milked on baby's account, otherwise the milk was horrid owing to their milking in dirty things which I should think were seldom washed.

Leaving the lakes, they set off on their march towards Thibet, as the real object of this leave was for Tom to shoot bear. The baby, who was not well, was carried in a *dhooley* on the first stage, while Tom walked and Jeanette shared a pony with the nurse. Jeanette enjoyed the marches and the camps' scenery; very beautiful, with good flowers, large white jasmine, blue monkshood, yellow Cape lilies, wild roses climbing "high up the trees". But always the difficulty about milk. "Today, Sweeper seized a beautiful goat and brought it to us. The owner came nearly weeping and brought another which he said he would lend us for a month."

They met some friends, which was enjoyable, but the camp was made hideous by the smell of 20 dead sheep and a dead horse discovered nearby, and two of their servants ran away but were brought back. "It would have been very awkward to have been two servants short", remarked Jeanette in her diary. The smell of dead animals had made Tom "quite seedy" and they were all glad of a rest

Leaving the Sind Valley, they crossed the Nojila Pass and several glaciers. While traversing one of these, there was a noise as of thunder and a huge boulder tore down the hillside, narrowly missing the baby and nurse.

It was this incident and the snow and increasingly hard conditions of Little Thibet that first made Jeanette wonder if these were suitable surroundings for her daughter. Provisions were running short and the coolies bringing fresh supplies were late in arriving. "Quantities of goats and sheep about, but cannot get them. Have to seize them and pay for them. Man came and told us with clasped hands that he would give us any amount of milk (which he has not done) if we would not take his sheep". The supplies eventually arrived and Tom went off on a shoot, to return with the skin of a fine bear, but "quite done up". The cook was "done up too and said he must leave, also the *khitmatghar* who arrived in tears saying his mother was dead. "Of course this is nonsense", said Jeanette. She was almost certainly right in her assessment of a favourite plea, corresponding to the office boy's grandmother. Tom went off on another shoot, accompanied by a very good *shikhari* (native hunter), who returned with some delicious fish he had tickled and, even more welcome, a large washing jug full of milk. The owner was angry, "but the *shikhari* just collared the goats and insisted upon them being milked", records a grateful Jeanette.

They had to travel over very bad country and cross several glaciers. Rosa was all right, carried wrapped in a blanket and sound asleep on the *shikhari*'s back. The going was so tough that Jeanette and the nurse each had a man to help them. The poor nurse disliked the whole proceeding and when they had to scramble down hills slippery with dry grass, she "with her big sun hat, black elastic under her chin, dress pinned up high anyhow and her long flannel petticoat showing, took her man's hand, running down the glacier and screaming loudly at the same time".

Tom went off on trek, leaving his wife, child and the nurse to spend a boring two days without him. In these odd surroundings, Jeanette records that she learnt to make pastry. There was champagne on their wedding aniversary and "a lovely bouquet of white flowers on the table". They were not without domestic

9

troubles, as the bearer finally left and two coolies bringing rice were drowned. Expenditure accounts tell us that sheep cost one rupee eight annas, eggs four annas a dozen, and fowls the same amount each. On the march back to Kashmir, they were invited to dine with a Major and Mrs. Hanna, who had come to camp near the Wards, a comfort to Jeanette, as Tom had again left her to go after bear. Jeanette had to arrive alone, making excuses for Tom who had not yet returned, and, as it turned out, for herself also, as her clocks were all an hour fast and she arrived correspondingly early to surprise her horrified hostess in curling pins. She was not as enchanted by Srinagar as many have been before and since. It was, she says, "a filthy smelly city". She had a poor opinion of the Kashmiris too, "awful liars, you cannot believe a word they say, they are also great cowards".

Rosa's nurse, however, appears to have enjoyed Srinagar more than her employers did, as on her day off, she went into the city and failed to return at the arranged time of 6 pm. At 10 pm, the Wards were so worried that Tom had to go and look for her. Perhaps it was exhaustion after her prolonged outing that made the nurse a little careless next day, for she did not observe till there was a sudden splash that baby Rosa had climbed out of her bed "for the very first time, and as it was near the side, she went straight into the water".

After their Kashmir trip, the Wards returned to Murree and then to England, via Cairo and Shepheard's Hotel, from the windows of which they watched the funeral procession of Ismail Pasha. "It took one hour to pass, in which there were no stoppages—oxen—camels —native regiments—hundreds and hundreds of natives walking—all the blind men in Cairo—the principal people of Cairo—the Khedive Lord Cromer etc. etc. etc.—the coffin and women behind it who howled and cried."

Army life is an immensely long plait, whose many strands weave in and out from one side to the other and back again. Henry Wood and his family lived in Murree, as did the Wards a generation later Tom Ward, then a general, played a part in the discovery and identification of the body of Bernard Grissell, husband of Olive, and Henry's son-in-law. In the third generation the baby Rosa, having grown safely to woman's estate, in spite of falling boulders and nea drowning, to distinguish herself in many fields of public service, gave her mother's diary to Henry's granddaughter for inclusion in this book.

Zoe Proctor preceded Tom and Jeanette by ten years when she went to stay with Colonel and Mrs. Berkeley, he being at that time Temporary Resident to the Maharajah of Kashmir. The journey entertained and interested Zoe enormously. The first stopping place was at a palace, built by the Maharajah for the visit of the Prince of Wales, and where pride of place was given, among beautiful Indian hangings and carpets, to a hideous ornament decorated with the announcement "A present from Margate", and a shell-box from Southend. The Valley of Kashmir was a never-to-be-forgotten sight, filled with purple and white irises that bent in waves before the wind. The Resident had a most luxurious houseboat at his disposal, with rose silk curtains dividing the boat into sleeping rooms at night and drawn back during the day so that the passengers could sit at ease and admire the flowers and the blossoming fruit trees, as 60 boatmen, uniformed in red and white, rowed the boat with heart-shaped paddles made of the *papier mâché* for which Kashmir was famous.

Zoe, like Jeanette, was horrified at the crowding and dirt in which the townspeople lived, though she rejoiced in the crafts, the silver and brass work and the exquisite hand-painted *papier mâché* objects, boxes, pen cases, blotters, mirrors, lamps, trays and countless other ornaments that decorated the houses of so many for generations. The great thrill for Zoe was winning the prize for her painting of flowers in her section of the Amateur Artists Club. Though her wardrobe must have been extended since the days when she wore her confirmation dress for best, the prize money came in handy. A *dhurzee*, working on the Berkeley verandah, ran her up a brown dress, the material of which cost her all she had won, but gave great satisfaction. Her return to Murree in the heat of August coincided with an outbreak of cholera, which terrified her, and no wonder, since coffin followed coffin down the Mall, each preceded by the "Dead March in Saul".

Soon after this, Colonel Proctor retired and the family income was even more reduced than it should have been. The Colonel had, while still a subaltern, backed a bill for a brother officer who had failed to pay so that Proctor was left with a lifetime's load of debt. On her father's retirement, Zoe went again to the Berkeleys, where she played tennis with the Indian princeling of whom Colonel Berkeley was in charge, and went to her first and only dance. She describes her performance on the floor as painful to her partner and herself, and the only other she ever attended was some years later in London, when she chaperoned her sister.

The three elder Proctor sisters had a very gay time, but Zoe was considered too young to take part, although her grandmother had been married and become a mother at a corresponding age. She was allowed to go to one very grand ball given by the Maharajah of Gwalior, where the garden was illuminated by thousands of lighted wicks floating in their saucers of oil, and the jewels worn by His Highness "quite eclipsed the treasured ornaments of the white women". Annie, Alice and Mary wore tight-laced ball gowns but Zoe, who describes the event with no trace of envy, wore her white confirmation dress. She was also allowed to watch her sisters and their beaux dancing in the open air to the music of the Regimental Bands in the Club gardens. The dance floor was a large area of tightly-stretched cloth and the dancers waltzed, swung into the Grand Chain of the Lancers, or sped with deft and practised feet through the intricate steps of the Highland Schottische under the huge, high moon and the softer light of lanterns hanging in the trees.

In 1911 occurred one of the greatest pieces of pageantry India ever saw. The Delhi Durbar was the occasion of the visit of King George V and Queen Mary to His Majesty's Indian Empire and every British man, woman and child participated in a lesser or greater degree. Captain Bernard Grissell, the Norfolk Regiment, was one of the ADCs appointed for the event, which meant that his golden-haired wife, Olive, had a splendid time at the Viceregal Balls and camps and shoots which were so much a feature of the royal visit. There were parties for the children too, and at one of these the Viceroy, Lord Hardinge, weighed down with garlands of marigolds presented at every *tomasha* (celebration) to people of importance took one of them off and put it round a Grissell child's neck. The sharp smell of the tight-strung blossoms dangling to her knees was the first flower-smell she ever remembered.

Smells! They are what bring places back to those who have left them, India especially. Do many British children know what a dead tiger smells like? The Grissell children did, as they watched the great beast their father had shot brought into the compound, slung by his legs on a pole and then arranged on the ground to have his photograph taken. The smell of the earth soaking up the first rain of the monsoon, of watered lucerne, of roasting *gram* (chickpea) from the servants' godowns, of tobacco smoked on the roadside in a communal pipe and the tremendous, heady, bitter smell of something in the Simla bazaar—you never forgot and you longed to smell it again. Sometimes, it nearly came back in the smell of autumn leaves burning, or varnish. or packing cases, but never the same.

A considerable number of army families spent the years of the 1914–18 war in India. They found themselves in an unpleasant predicament when it was over and were unable to get home owing to a shortage of troopships. The fearful influenza was as much of a menace as it was in Europe and Indians and British died in great numbers. But all that passed too and for the army, life settled back to normal. Girls came out on the Fishing Fleet and older relatives came visiting too. Among these latter was Aunt Louise (see p. 211), whose favourite nephew, Captain Green, was serving with her beloved KSLI. The Greens, temporarily stationed in Karachi, had only a small flat, but Aunt Louise cheerfully camped in a tent on the roof in preference to going to a hotel. She returned to Delhi with them and was given her customary enthusiastic welcome by all ranks and both sexes. Officers who passed into the Staff College during their service in India went to Quetta instead of Camberley. One officer described the place as "Aldershot gone septic", though this was not the general opinion. But at 3 am on the morning of May 29th, 1935, in the space of three minutes, the city was devastated by an earthquake, which caused many deaths and great destruction.

By this date, it had become possible to fly to India, or to be more accurate, to make the seven days' journey by part air/part train, with no night-flying and landing every four hours or so to refuel.

It is doubtful if many of the soldiery or any of their wives realised that their days in India were numbered. Certainly those who went out in 1938 had no idea that they were making history simply by arriving, unpacking and settling into cantonment life as the last army generation to do so. It was all so ordinary, so established: Camberley, Catterick, Colchester set amid cannas, hibiscus and queen of the night, with no servant problems and a lovely, leisurely life of morning bridge and tea parties and the Club. The Club, that pivot of cantonment life, with its tennis courts, the children's playground, the Bar, the ballroom, the billiards room and the library and the regimental bands playing in the evening.

Except for the occasional shopping expedition, there was no need to stir outside cantonments and no need to learn the language, as one could always find a bearer who spoke English. No wonder the British army wife was regarded as a rather inferior being by her counterpart in the Indian army and no wonder her servants habitually cheated her.

She deserved no better and sometimes not as good as she got. In paying tribute to Mahomed Yusef, who served the Bamfield family for more than four years as bearer, it is impossible to speak too highly, or even highly enough of someone who deserves to be remembered as Kipling remembered Gunga Din. The contractor supplied everything for sale or on hire that any member of any regiment could possibly want or need. The same contractor took charge of "his" regiment whenever they went to India. Supplied by the regimental contractor, Mahomed presented his credentials in the form of two or three "chits", letters of recommendation from previous employers. The fact that there were only two or three of them spoke for the fact that he was a good servant, for he was not young. The chits themselves were so good that it seemed they must somehow be bogus. According to each of his employers, the man was a paragon of every virtue: loyal, honest, clean, efficient, and they would none of them have parted with him if they had not been leaving India. It was surely a risk to take him on, as so much adulation from white men would almost certainly have gone to his head.

While Major Bamfield, the Royal Welch Fusiliers, and his wife were debating the matter, Mahomed Yusef put the chits back into his pocket and took charge of the family, a position they never had any wish to deprive him of. He was a slight, middle-aged man with a stoop and a Charlie Chaplin moustache and there was one marked difference between him and most Indian servants. He laughed. Without ever becoming familiar, he could enjoy and even make jokes and he told the Bamfield children splendid, enthralling stories of Sultana the Dacoit long before the account of the capture of this colourful character appeared in a book by Jim Corbett.

When the Royal Welch Fusiliers were sent home in 1941 and the women and children were not allowed to travel, Mahomed Yusef told his master that he would never leave the family while they remained in India. So faithfully did he keep his word that he would not even take his annual leave to return for two weeks to his own village. At his suggestion, the *khitmatghar* was dismissed as an unnecessary expense, and he did all the housework and waiting himself without asking for the modest rise in wages that brought his monthly pay from 50 rupees to 70 rupees. Well aware that he could have had the whole family under his thumb (the Bamfields never handled money: all cash was handed over to him and dished out on demand!), he never became impertinent or presumptuous. The only privilege he assumed without asking permission was to turn the wireless on to listen to the war news on All-India Radio every morning before breakfast. When the family left India, he escorted them to Bombay and salaamed his final good-byes—or so they thought. Next morning, while the ship was still at anchor, he was found on board against all wartime regulations, hugging the youngest child who had always been his special "baba", with tears running down his face. Then he disappeared. *Salaam aleikum!* ("Peace be with you!"—the traditional Mahomedan greeting).

Veronica Bamfield, the granddaughter of Henry Wood, was one of the lucky few on whom India lays a dark, jewelled hand, the warmth of whose touch never grows cold to those who have felt it. And it happened quite suddenly in the unlikely surroundings of a wayside railway halt. The journey of the 2nd Battalion, the Royal Welch Fusiliers, from Bombay to Lucknow with the regimental goat as one of the passengers, took two days and a night, and before dark at the end of the first day, there was a stop of an hour to allow humans and goat to take exercise. From the few mud houses near the halt, children scampered up to stare and grin and ask for money, though these were not the harrowing professional child-beggars who hung on to the steps of trains as they moved out of stations, one hand clinging to the rail, the other still stretched out beseeching, jumping off seconds before the trains gathered speed. These were village children, the first the army children had seen at close quarters and they stared at each other. The evening air was warm, the light still, and suddenly Veronica knew with absolute certainty that she had come back to a country, not that she knew, but that knew her. She was safe, protected. Then, within a few days, she found the smell again! It came pouring out of the new, badly-made *almirah* (cup-board) in the bedroom when she opened the doors. She was back in the furniture-makers' part of the Simla bazaar, and time was noth-ing. Powerful, sharp, bittersweet, it embraced her. "Welcome" it told her, "You've come back. You're home".

She was lucky. She knew a little of what India could have been for so many, to whom it was simply a good-time place. A little, not enough and too late. Nowhere in the world have so many oppor-tunities been missed as were missed by the army wives in India. They took so much trouble to bring Aldershot, Catterick and Colchester to Lucknow, Quetta, Bareilly and all those other places, as they sat in their chintzy drawing-rooms and went down to the Club to get the newest English library books, handed to them by the *babu* whose English they laughed at. They never wondered what he thought of them for not bothering to learn a word of Hindustani. What did they all think, the *babus* and the shopkeepers, the railway clerks, the *tonga wallahs* they swore at, or the high-caste Indians who could have taught them so much and whom they never made any attempt to get to know because they were "natives"? It is only amazing that they put up with the ignorance and arrogance for so long, ignorance and arrogance for which there was no excuse as there had been for the grandmothers. For this was the modern

generation, born of emancipated stock, and whose health was
stronger and better looked-after. General John Jacob was right. The
army wife never really acclimatised herself to India and there is no
doubt that boredom, though often unrecognised, crippled her
character in all sorts of ways. She wasted her time and her often not
inconsiderable talents. She learnt nothing and contributed nothing.
We should be ashamed. All of us.

A number of wives of officers and other ranks went to join their
husbands after the South African War, two of Henry Wood's
daughters, Olive and Hazel, being among them. Olive, accompanied
by her mother and her future brother-in-law who acted as best man,
went out to be married in Cape Town cathedral in 1906. Another
was Mrs. Mitford (she who had disapproved of troopships—see
p. 38) who set out to join her husband, Colonel Mitford of the East
Surrey Regiment, in 1903. On arrival in Cape Town, where they
had to wait a week before proceeding to Pretoria, the family stayed
in one hotel and the two maids in another more suitable to their
station in life. On the long journey over the Karoo to Pretoria, the
girls were cautioned against leaning out of the window because of
dangerous sparks blown back from the engine. The military cantonment in Pretoria was a very pleasant place in which to live, with car-
peted floors and ornaments everywhere. There was the superb
Transvaal country to ride over, the flowering trees, the birds and the
splendour of the skies at dawn and sunset. There was a good deal of
entertaining, picnics, dances and dinner parties. At one of the latter
Olive Wood, as hostess, stared in speechless surprise as her white-
uniformed native servants handed round the dishes, their gleaming
ebony foreheads decorated with the round coloured labels removed,
unknown to herself, from her Coat's cotton reels.

The Mitfords lived in one of the corrugated-iron houses built at
the turn of the century, some of which still survive and look
strangely exotic amidst all the concrete high-rise. The Swiss maid
soon found an admirer in a young Boer farmer and married him,
moving into a spotless farmhouse which the Mitford girls enjoyed
visiting. Many of their friends lived in tents, huge affairs furnished
like houses with drawing-room, dining-room and bedrooms. Young

Jocelyn Mitford remembers being taken by her father into Pretoria to see the funeral of President Kruger. The crowds were so dense that it was difficult to see anything and she missed the cortège entirely, but did see the generals and statesmen riding by while all around her, the Boer women in their big cotton *kapjies* (sun-bonnets) wept for Oom Paul.

Gibraltar was a popular foreign posting and young Mrs. Burton, wife of colour sergeant Clifford Burton, the Royal Welch Fusiliers, was pleased to be going there, though not so pleased when she found that her husband was going on ahead and she had to follow alone. The voyage was a happy one, but she was glad to think of the end of it and of being met by her husband. But there was not a sign of him on that sunny day in 1931 as the *Orford* drew into Gibraltar Harbour.

Several disconsolate wives disembarked to climb into the transport sent to meet them, an army lorry with wooden forms in the back as a concession to comfort. They chugged up to Buena Vista, disinclined to admire the magnificent view over the Mediterranean. Women got down at intervals and were taken to their quarters. Irene was the last and she viewed hers with dismay. There was just one room, with a bedroom and kitchen leading off it. The lavatory was approached via the kitchen. No bath or any facilities for washing except the kitchen sink. Everything was filthy, including the safe hanging on an outside wall, their only larder and crawling with ants. An inconsequential, but none the less alarming, thought flashed immediately to mind. Where was she to put the top layer of the wedding cake, carefully packed and transported against a possible future christening?

She had never read about the wives in the Crimea, who had to combat ants so large and so belligerent that they carried portions of food away, but it was clear to her that her wedding cake was in grave peril. The coal-boys brought up some ration coal which she signed for and took in. Better get a fire going, heat some water and clean out that ghastly lavatory. By the time she had finished, discovering with relief that at least the flush worked, she was summoned to take in stores arrived from the NAAFI. Flour, fat, sugar and some apples decided her to make an apple pie. Her husband arrived from the Orderly Room to ask if she was all right, and to say he couldn't stop, that he'd get his dinner in Mess and what was she going to have?

This casual, to say the least, treatment of wives was a well-known characteristic of the Royal Welch Fusiliers—a regiment that considered its wives lucky to have married into it. And why not? No other regiment wore the Flash, that knot of black ribbons, that "relic of many a siege and sack—points a moral and adorns the back" in memory of their being the last regiment to abandon the powdered wig and the black silk bag that kept the queue of the wig from marking the red coats. What other regiment had such a splendidly caparisoned goat from the royal herd as its regimental mascot, owned the keys of Corunna, kept a harpist to play at guest nights, and boasted a colonel who was an elected bard? No other regimental wives ate a raw leek in public on the first St. David's Day of their married life and gave the toast in Welsh to "Dewi Sant". Any girl who married into such a distinguished regiment must walk humbly, not so much with the Lord her God, but in the wake of her earthly lord and master, be he colonel, private or any of the ranks between. No Royal Welch Fusilier wife expected any consideration. A civilian who knew the regiment well remarked that he reckoned its women qualified for danger money.

But Irene, being newly wed and inexperienced, did think herself so entitled on that day in Gibraltar as she watched her husband bustle off to his good dinner, leaving her to burst into tears. She was rescued from her woeful plight by the sergeant-major's wife, who arrived with her two daughters, Betty and Winnie. They dragged the issue mattress from the verandah where it had been dumped and Mrs. Sergeant-Major sent a message to her husband, telling him to come along quickly with a screwdriver. Packing cases were undone, bed linen and blankets extracted, and Irene, encouraged by the fact that the bed was made up and the place looked a bit more homely, got the kettle going and they all had a cup of tea. The day ended better than it had begun, with the sergeant-major's wife cooking supper for everybody.

Before long, Irene moved to a better quarter, with a decent cooking range, a bath (in the kitchen, with a lid that fitted over it to make a table) and a boiler for laundry. This was done once a week by a

Spanish girl, who came over the border from La Linea. Sophie worked for several families for a daily wage of 1s. 6d. and her lunch. Everything dried very quickly and the household washing and ironing was finished in a day. Fresh water was scarce and every drop used for personal washing during the week was saved and used on washday. Coloured things were washed in the bath and the whites boiled in the boiler. Sophie brought her own charcoal iron and the fuel which heated it from the inside was provided by the employers. Irene had her own flat irons and Sophie heated these on the primus stove, that indispensable part of army married life. Irene had an oven, which fitted on top of the primus and this meant they could save the ration coal and have a fire in the living-room in the evening.

"Methylaty" and "Parafiny" were brought round for sale every Friday by an old Gibraltarian, and another brought drinking water in a cart. A week's supply cost 1s. 6d. Fresh water was issued on ration, but had to be boiled before drinking. Irene had 30s. out of her husband's £2 pay (after stoppages) to last her the week. Rations were issued under the same system as in Britain. Meat, nearly always beef, twice a week, flour, salt, pepper, sugar and some vegetables were issued daily. Every Thursday, Irene took the money in lieu, 2½d. for each commodity. The amount due was held over till the end of the month and the total sum helped buy things to vary the ration diet which were expensive as they were exported from Britain. If food and housekeeping money ran out before pay day, they bought one 10d. supper from the NAAFI between them, which they shared after reheating it on the primus. The favourite was liver, onions and mash and another vegetable, often the dried peas that were known as "sloppy doppies".

There was a good deal of social life for all families of all ranks. The officers and their wives and families hunted foxes in the corkwoods, much as the Duke of Wellington had done in times of war. Picnics by the sea, boat trips, visits to see the famous apes, excursions into Spain, and the excitement when the ships came in. It all added up to the good life. It seemed to an army wife of those days that if you lived in Gibraltar you would see most of your friends on their way to and from India. Gib was a great place for people simply turning up for a few hours. When the luxuries arrived from home, the shops were crowded with women buying table-treats like kippers, bacon and real marmalade. Local meat was good and fruit and vegetables excellent and cheap.

Hong Kong and Shanghai were popular stations too. The exotic Chinese landscape, unlike that of any other country, the blossom and the snows and the people all so unlike anything anywhere else made a two years' posting an exotic experience. Children were happy, cared for with enigmatic tenderness by the amah. Meek and gentle, moving softly in her black cloth shoes, her thin, sometimes bent body neatly clothed in blue cotton coat and trousers, she went about her work with an efficiency that deprived her mistress of anxiety and washed and ironed clothes as beautifully as any French lady's maid.

One of the real luxuries about life in China was the cheapness of clothes and shoes. The excellence of Chinese tailors and shoemakers is proverbial and legendary. And there were so many of them tucked into their little shops, advertising themselves with delightful pidgin English notices. The most famous, quoted by the writer Daniel Varé, proclaimed that "Ladies have fits upstairs". They were superb, if unimaginative, copyists and it is always claimed that, unless instructed otherwise, they would take great trouble to fake a mend in a suit or dress. China gave the army wife a better way of life than she was likely to lead anywhere else, socially and domestically, during her husband's service. Her house was kept spotless by the amah, the "boy", or, if she could afford it, both. These never needed chasing as the Indian servants did, and it would have been demeaning for her and to them if she lifted a finger to help. She may not have had as easy access to kippers and bacon as in Gib, but since China was so far away from Britain everything necessary to the British army's way of life was meticulously arranged and catered for.

No wife, or soldier husband either for that matter, bothered with Chinese. There were too many different dialects, the pronunciation was impossible, and pidgin English had become a language in its own right. Parcels went home at Christmas or for family birthdays containing the drawn-thread table napkins, the appliquéed hand towels and bedspreads, the brocade slippers and purses, the bracelets and rings in coral, enamel or jade, that have become part of so many British households as family souvenirs and even heirlooms.

Life could sometimes be troubled in China. Colonel Robinson, commanding the 1st Battalion The King's Shropshire Light Infantry had his wife and children with him in Hong Kong when plague broke out in 1894. The colonel kept a diary in which all matters pertaining to the Regiment including the progress of the plague were recorded, but there is never a mention of his own or any other family. It can be assumed that Mrs. Robinson in her capacity of colonel's lady did a good deal of visiting, calming and possibly consoling among the wives of the officers and the other ranks whose situation was precarious and whose anxiety must have been great, but as far as the colonel and his record were concerned they did not exist. Nevertheless Mrs. Robinson has a unique if modest memorial dating from those anxious days. Among other trophies in a glass case in the regimental museum in Shrewsbury lies a Chinese umbrella made of heavy waxed paper, Mrs. Robinson's umbrella brought home and handed over after their parents' death by the two ladies known as "the Miss Robinsons"—devoted worshippers in the church from which the Polehamptons had set out for Lucknow, and known to generations of children taught by Miss Marjorie in Sunday School—who had been the little daughters of the colonel when the plague was raging.

The occasional typhoon was dangerous and alarming, especially one time when the men were all away on a manoeuvre and the wives feared for the safety of their property and even their lives during the whole of one long night.

Life in Bermuda, Britain's oldest colony, was pleasant but expensive. Henry Wood's daughter, Olive, who lived there in the 1930s as the wife of the Governor, Lieut.-General Sir Thomas Astley Cubitt worried over the housekeeping of the junior married officers and other ranks, with cauliflowers costing as much as 1s. 8d. each. She and her daughters, spent five happy years in Government House and one of the daughters returned as the wife of Major Eric Russell Grenadier Guards, to the old-fashioned charm of whitewashed army quarters, with never a motor-car to break into the leisurely way of life. All houses on the island had tanks on the roofs to collect the only available water. Drinking water was imported and arrived by boat.

Most of the army wives stationed in Singapore were evacuated before its surrender in February 1942. One of those who stayed behind was Ruth Russell-Roberts, whose husband, Dennis, had transferred from The King's Shropshire Light Infantry to the 3/11th Sikh Regiment. Colonel Russell-Roberts was with his regiment up-country, their little daughter had been taken back to England by friends, and Ruth worked first at RAF HQ and then as a sergeant clerk in the casualties section of 2nd Echelon. At the surrender, however, she was obliged to leave and boarded the SS *Mata Hari* on February 12th, 1942. As she and her husband said goodbye, she said "My best hope for you is that you will become a prisoner of war". "And for you", he answered, "we must pray it will be Java, then Australia, and eventually England."

That best hope was fulfilled for Dennis but not for Ruth.

The scenes at the embarkation were reminiscent of the old days of the ballot, only this time it was the husbands who had to stay behind. A wife with her baby in her arms declared she would jump overboard if her husband went ashore. When it became clear that she meant what she threatened, the ship's captain enrolled the sergeant as a clerk and took him aboard. One child got separated from his mother, who was taken to a different ship, and one distraught woman hunted for two of her three children from whom she had become parted on the quay. Five hundred passengers, including 132 women and children, plus 100 British and Australian army nurses, went on board and before long, they picked up 120 survivors from another ship.

There were three flush lavatories in the officers' quarters and these were reserved for the women and children. The other passengers and crew used native-type squat pans. There was a total of three lifeboats in poor condition. They were bombed from a height of 12,000 feet by two Japanese planes that dropped six bombs each, but, miraculously, she was not hit. Passengers lived and slept wherever they could find space, as accommodation was utterly inadequate in spite of the generosity of the ship's officers in giving up their cabins. Chased by the Japanese, the captain tried to get to Palembang, Sumatra, but was forced to surrender to the enemy and anchored at Muntok.

Here, the women and children were housed, together with the exhausted survivors from 60 other ships, in the Coolie Assembly Station, sleeping in rows on concrete slabs so that they immediately nicknamed it "Macfisheries". From there, they were taken across the Banka Straits to Sumatra and up-river to Palembang. Life in a prison camp for this beautiful girl was, in certain respects, more difficult than for some of the women. Her remarkable looks, her wit and her prowess at all sports, as well as flying, had opened doors for her everywhere, but those doors had not led into the kitchen or to make-do-and-mend classes. A friend took her in hand and taught her to sew and knit and cook, and was of great help to her in her difficulty of living under the strain of her handicap of deafness.

The camp at Palembang consisted of artisans' houses, built along either side of two streets. They were quite large, with two or three bedrooms, dining- and living-rooms, but not large enough for the comfort of the 25 women allotted to each house. Mosquitoes, lack of wood for cooking and no soap were some of the daily trials, as well as no hats or shoes, both of which made moving about in a hot sun painful and dangerous. Some local tradesmen were allowed into camp and it was possible to buy lengths of cloth, needles and cotton. These were all women used to leading pleasant social lives, and once the chores were over, time hung heavy. Hunger took hold and a longing for cosmetics, irreplaceable once they were finished. Many of them had a certain amount of jewellery, which changed hands for food and other commodities. Church services were well attended and gave great comfort, being conducted by an English missionary. There was no lack of entertainment either. Bridge fours used home-made cards and Mah Jong players did the same, making whole sets. There were singsongs to a treasured piano and concerts and theatricals.

Colonel Russell-Roberts, himself a prisoner in Changi, Singapore wrote afterwards how much worse it was for the women than for the men, because though the conditions for both were hideous, with the same privations and uncertainty as to the fate of their families since communication was forbidden except for the rare postcard to the United Kingdom, and loneliness and anxiety were everyone's bed-fellows, yet the men managed never to be without hidden home-made wireless sets and were thus in touch with the world outside.

But with Ruth and her companions, there was nothing (writes her husband). A curtain of silence had fallen between them and the rest of the world, through which not even the smallest ray of hope could travel. And this agony of silence remained with them throughout. We who think we suffered in Changi should remember this and be grateful.

These women prisoners were not allowed to send postcards for the first 18 months and Ruth did not know that her daughter had safely arrived in England for two years. Even so, local messages got through between prisoners in a remarkable way, smuggled usually in the ration truck. Ruth, after some difficult and dangerous negotia-tions with a Japanese, smuggled a letter to her husband, who she was convinced was alive and in Changi. In the New Year of 1943, the women were all moved to another and much worse camp near Palembang. It was cold, damp and 60 shared each hut with two bathrooms in which the long, cement open drains served as lavatories. In 1944, letters came from England, and American Red Cross parcels "arrived from apparently nowhere". There were good things to eat, even if only in very small quantities. Then the whole camp was moved again, back to Muntok.

In Changi, Dennis Russell-Roberts prevailed upon a "Japanese who was different", to use his own description, to take a letter to Ruth at Palembang, not knowing that she had been transferred. It reached her eventually, as she lay very ill with Banka fever, too weak to read it herself. She listened to the long, the only letter her hus-band had been able to send her, delivered now only a very short time before the prisoners from Changi would be freed and those from Muntok flown to Singapore. She listened, smiled and went to sleep. And did not wake.

Most stations were good, at any rate in retrospect, but the time came when the last had to be left, the collected souvenirs of years packed up and labelled "not wanted on voyage" for home. The same troopship that took you out often took you back again. Home. You were going home and home is where the heart is. Or is it? Can you ever say again that your heart is whole? That it belongs to any single place? "Partir c'est mourir un peu", "Every time I say good-bye, I die a little". Very true, sometimes terribly poignantly as when the farewell posy of flowers is laid on a small grave, or when you know that the return will be emptier because of a parent who has died.

Home. England, Ireland, Scotland, Wales. Eldorado and Far Cathay, when you were ill or homesick, the Land of Promise you sometimes thought you might never see again. Home, the place you came from but to which, often in sad surprise, you never fully return. Too much of your life, your memory, your heart is left behind in all those other places. Suns will scorch and moons ride high and bright, winds will sigh through mountain pines or whiplash over deserts and you will not be there to see. Voices singing half-remembered languages will steal into your ears as you fall asleep. Taste and smell will sometimes betray you for a fleeting second into thinking you are back again. You didn't matter in any of those places. Not really. No-one will remember you've ever been, though you will always be a little homesick for places that have forgotten you. That is the private tragedy of many army wives. Home is nowhere.

References to Chapter 6

Complete Indian Housekeeper and Cook, F. A. Steel, Heinemann, 1887
Life and Yesterday, Z. Proctor, Favil Press
Spotlight on Singapore, D. Russell-Roberts, Times Press, 1963

7. Sickness and Health

"IT'S A GOOD life if you don't weaken" groaned the subaltern with a hangover, and his complaint could be a fair assessment of the day-to-day life of the army family for many generations. In the bad old times, you got on well enough as long as you were well. Fall sick, and your lot was dire indeed. You died as you had lived in the barrack-room or following the column to war, and in between it took all your resources to keep up with the tough going.

As with so much else, it was the scandal of the Crimean administration that brought about better conditions. News of the nightmare existence of degradation led by about 300 women and children left behind when the army moved up to Varna, living in cellars under the Turkish barracks which had been taken over as a hospital in Scutari reached a horrified Britain. A fund was started to do what could be done to relieve their sufferings. The Reverend Doctor and Lady Alicia Blackwood travelled out at their own expense to offer help, and Lady Alicia was asked by Miss Nightingale to take charge of the women living in the cellars. Lady Alicia, and Mrs. Bracebridge who arrived in Scutari soon after the Blackwoods, tackled their near impossible task with boundless energy, courage and sincerely Christian principles. Their presence and its amazingly successful results was an enormous relief to Florence Nightingale. She was well aware of the women's plight, but was obliged to adopt her apparently callous attitude towards them for the very simple reason that she had neither time nor supplies to divert from the men she had been sent out to care for.

Mrs. Bracebridge and her husband had travelled widely and no doubt encountered poverty and filth before, if only from a distance. It is certain that neither they, nor the Blackwoods, had met conditions like these. The cellars were open cesspits, rats abounded, the only bedding for those lucky enough to have any at all was sodden sacking. Bed bugs, lice and enormous rats carried the infections of cholera and fever, while in the cellar, hopefully but hopelessly set aside as a hospital, the dead were removed when it was noticed life had left them to make room for the births and more deaths that would take place on the same filthy mattress.

The Times, which by its reporting of the war did much to better the domestic lot of the army, sent a representative to administer the fund organised by the paper, and the reports he sent back were hair-raising. Forty-eight women, many of them with children, were herded in one small room; the dead were shuffled into nameless graves because people did not know their neighbour by name. Fighting, prostitution, and above all stealing, were the means of obtaining arrack, the strong local spirit that was the only palliative in cold, hunger, pain and fear. These women did not take kindly to the do-gooders. Talk about Christian virtues, however gentle and tactful, meant nothing to them. What they wanted were money and clothes and these were the things, in their opinion, that the ladies and gentlemen should have brought them. One of the better class among the women was employed as a servant by the Blackwoods, but even in her extremity and with a chance of better and more comfortable living, she flatly refused to cook, and did the cleaning and washing she consented to do unwillingly.

Nevertheless, these amateurs persisted and gradually the fruits of their toil began to be apparent. A laundry was set up and the women who worked in it received regular wages. There was a nursery attached where the workers could have their babies looked after, and there was a hospital with a doctor sent out from England. The Free Gift Store opened two mornings a week and sold goods sent from England or provisions bought locally with money from charitable organisations. There were better cooking arrangements for the sick, and from the bales of cloth and flannel sent out, the women were able to make clothes for themselves and their children. But the better conditions brought their own problems. Improved feeding and housing resulted in better health and restored the women's self-respect, but made them more discontented with their lot, more demanding, more insistent that they should have more pay, more food, more of everything. Lady Alicia, quick to realise that the little pious talks she gave in the beginning were not what was wanted, left the women's spiritual welfare to the Almighty, and slaved on with Mrs. Bracebridge and other helpers to achieve more order out of chaos than would have been thought possible.

That the army owes an irredeemable debt to Florence Nightingale for her reforms is undeniable, but even as early as 1843 the condition of the soldier's family in sickness was a matter of concern. This was not because the health of the women and children, as such, was thought to be important, but because they could, in sickness, be a danger to the health of the army. An outbreak of smallpox among the families in Chatham had caused a colonel to write a letter in a very shaky hand with an unreadable signature to the Secretary at War. In it, he states it to be his opinion that it would be advisable to have a hospital in which to nurse such cases. The Secretary at War referred the matter to the Director General, adding in his turn that if a hospital for infectious diseases were built, a ward might be allotted for women and children "on the clear and distinct ground of the safety of the health of the troops", and that "such an innovation must be strictly watched that it does not degenerate into abuse". The Treasury, for their part, seemed "inclined to limit the accordance to cases where the soldier would suffer from contact with infectious disease", though they were in agreement with the principle. The Secretary of State "has taken measures to regulate the admission of such patients as will have the effect of restricting the indulgence to those cases only where decency and propriety clearly demand the adoption of such arrangement". One can only be relieved that the writer of this letter went on to observe that "the cases of women in parturition are quite as urgent on the score of decency as cases of sickness; and even more so". This venture into compassionate sensitivity was offset by a further paragraph to the effect that the medical officer of any hospital admitting a woman was not to do so unless she was in possession of a certificate to the hospital caterer stating that she was in need of hospital treatment.

The struggle ding-donged for years. Where should the hospitals be built? And if women were to be admitted, which women? The answer to this seems an almost unbelievable combination of red tape and brutal stupidity. *Admission could only be granted to those women whose husbands were below the rank of sergeant.* In vain was it pointed out that this would cause great hardship to the sergeant, who, in view of his age, would almost certainly have a larger family than the private, and his living expenses would be correspondingly greater. In vain did the Duke of Cambridge, Commander-in-Chief of the army, with more concern for the lives of the men under him than his predecessor Wellington had shown, cross swords with Lord Panmure, Secretary of State for War. The Duke contended that *if* a woman were admitted to the hospitals, the charge for her food should not be stopped from the man's pay, that pay "being barely sufficient to maintain his own efficiency". The Duke went further and stated flatly that "the General Commander-in-Chief has no power, nor would it be expedient if he had, to authorise any deduction being made from the soldier's pay for the hospital accommodation of his family". He was opposed by the Treasury who, understandably it must be owned, felt that it would be wrong to expect the taxpayer to stand the cost. The one hospital which did actually admit families, Fort Pitt at Chatham, was obliged to close its Female Ward.

The Lock Hospital for Infectious Disease at Aldershot did admit women for the treatment of venereal disease, and issued a long and detailed report in 1870. From this, it would appear that all the women admitted were prostitutes, though it is possible, if somewhat unlikely, that the failure to mention wives might have been due to discretion. There had been an unusual amount of illness on the wards, which had complicated the treatment for venereal infections and "made it difficult to select an adequate number of women fit to attend the duties of the laundry and the kitchen, in addition to the other work of the Establishment". There was a regular annual increase in the number of patients to the male wards after the summer manoeuvres, when the prostitutes descended like locusts and lodged round the tented camps.

"Ladies of position" visited the women in the Lock Hospital and proved effective as an aid to the redemption of many of the unfortunates with whom "they held kindly conversation". Lady Hope Grant, wife of the Divisional Commander, was one of these. She procured "at her own expense" a temporary home for one of the patients prior to her lying-in.

This expectant mother was more fortunate than a Mrs. Walker, wife of a soldier serving overseas, who wrote to *The Times*. "I have nothing but my needle to depend on to provide for myself, one child, and another unborn. I have neither the money nor necessaries for my confinement". There were all too many Mrs. Walkers left behind without even the talent of fine sewing to earn them a pittance.

Out in the Crimea, two soldiers' wives were officially appointed as nurses by Miss Nightingale, Mrs. Evans and Mrs. Box, adding thus to their Crimean laurels (see pp. 68 and 75). Another woman with an army background did wonderful work in the Crimea. Mary Seacole was the Creole daughter of a Scottish army officer stationed in Jamaica. As a large, youngish, flamboyant, widow, she travelled widely after her shadowy husband's death and finished up in the Crimea. Determined to nurse the wounded, she put her high intelligence, considerable knowledge of medicine and nursing, as well as a sizable fortune, at the disposal of Miss Nightingale. The fine-boned, well-bred lady in her quiet grey dress looked across her desk at the mass of brightly-dressed, coffee-coloured humanity on the other side and turned all these offers down with glacial thanks.

Though hurt and very surprised, Mrs. Seacole was not one to shed any tears over spilt milk. She knew soldiers; she had known them all her life and helped to look after them in her mother's boarding house from her early girlhood. She was not allowed to nurse them, but nobody could stop her looking after them in the hotel she would build. So she took herself off to Balaclava, bribed two British sailors and a few Turkish workmen, and superintended the salvaging of wood from the wrecked ships in the harbour. In an amazingly short time, the British Hotel was built, with rooms to let and excellent cuisine. It was a well-run and respectable establishment: doors closed at 8 pm precisely, no Sunday business and no gambling. But Mother Seacole, as everybody called her, was down before daybreak to open the place and serve hot coffee to exhausted men returning from night duty, and to start cooking the good, nourishing food she prepared for the convalescents, roasting the chicken, beef and mutton, boiling the lobsters, spicing the wine, and moving her huge bulk with agility from stove to serving counter all through the long day. She even undertook party catering and had a private room upstairs which could be hired for private celebrations. She ordered

152 ON THE STRENGTH

her stores from England and paid good money for local produce. So she was never without anything except milk. This was unobtainable, and her "sons" had to have their coffee diluted with lumps of butter and their rice puddings made with water.

She loved them all and they loved her, many owing their return to health after wounds or fever to her good feeding and cheerful encouragement. As many again whispered their last messages home to her as they lay dying. She moved among the wounded, lying on the landing-stage waiting for the transports, wondering if they would live to see home again. They were encouraged and comforted by Mary Seacole, who wrapped them up against the cold in blankets of her own providing, or spread muslin nets made by herself over them to keep off the summer flies. They knew their whispered farewells to their loved ones would reach them, because "Mother" said so. The warmth of her clasp was comfort to a hand growing cold. She was a truly splendid woman, with a heart as large and as comfortable as her own hotel; but kind as she was to the soldier and hard as she worked on his behalf, there is no indication that she gave a thought to his wife.

One who did, and very unexpectedly, was Lord Raglan, the Commander-in-Chief. Riding out one day, he came upon the wife of a soldier in the 23rd Foot lying in a dugout improvised from a ditch, with a covering stretched over it, trying to keep herself and her newborn baby warm. Dismounting, he crawled inside the miserable shelter and talked with her. Then, deeply concerned, he returned to his own quarters and ordered a servant to take her provisions supplied by himself, and the rubber flannel-lined sleeping bag recently arrived from England. When she was on her feet and about again, the little wife from the Welsh valley found the means of sending her thanks and news of the baby's welfare to his lordship.

Officers and their wives paid little attention to the welfare of the other women, though Fanny did go and see one sick woman, recording in her journal that the poor soul's fever was so high that the heat of her body had dried the surrounding mud into cracks.

There was an enormous amount of coming and going to and from the Crimea. Officers' ladies jaunted out, accompanied by mountains of luggage, children, nurses and lady's maids, and mothers also went out to be near their sons. Deputy Commissary Adams writes home that "Mrs. Bolton and Augusta have taken lodgings about six miles from Scutari where Lawrence is stationed. She intends following wherever he goes, but I fear the old lady will find much inconvenience in doing so. Money however will accomplish great things and soften down many asperities." It did not soften quite enough in this case, for some weeks later Adams wrote again with the news that "Poor Mrs. Bolton is dead. Lawrence and Augusta have left on a week's leave".

"Mrs. Watts is here", he writes in another letter, "she has a servant with her, but what she will do if her husband moves I cannot imagine. It is no place for ladies and especially her, poor creature, who is liable to fits." Poor Mrs. Watts! Her husband was moved and feeling unable to endure loneliness as well as ill-health, she suggested to Mrs. de Fonblanque, another grass widow, that they might share a house till their husbands returned. Mrs. de Fonblanque, though herself averse to being on her own with only her child for company, fancied the idea of living with sad, epileptic Mrs. Watts even less, and took herself off to visit her father, the Consul General in Serbia. Mrs. Watts died soon after and her last days cannot have been happy.

Childbirth was hazardous to mother or child, or, all too often, both, but even more so for the army wife because she bore her children under so many varied and often adverse conditions. Emily Polehampton's baby died on January 8th, 1857 and Henry has left a heartrending description.

I was thinking how happy I was and saying to myself "I have a son" in all the languages I know . . . I found the nurse looking very blank . . . baby had just had a convulsive fit. I baptised the child . . . we thought it better not to tell Emmie of its illness. After a time, the doctor advised that she should be told. She took alarm at once, but soon recovered and became very composed . . . he was in his mother's bed nearly all the time.

Then the nurse took the baby over near the fire to warm him, but he gasped for breath a little and died. Emmie took him back into her arms and cried "till nurse took him away and laid him out in his basket cradle where Emmie could look into it". In the evening, she had an alarming hysterical fit and the doctor said it was of the greatest importance that the baby was taken away from her. For, "hanging over him and gazing intently on him as she never ceased to do was having a very bad effect on her weak state. She did not make much objection when I told her." When morning and the final parting came, "she had the coffin put where the cradle had been and placed him in it herself and put some little dark red roses of which she is very fond in his hands and on his breast; then she bravely covered him up and I carried him out and fastened down the coffin out of her hearing". Then Henry took his little boy to the graveyard in a closed carriage—"the only ride we shall ever have together".

Fifty-odd years later, Henry Wood's daughter, Olive, lost her first-born in a stillbirth in South Africa and her husband, like Henry Polehampton, took his son in a carriage to burial. From her bed, she heard the sounds of sad departure and one especially lingered in memory all her life. "If only someone had oiled the hinge of the gate", she said.

Her sister, Hazel, also married to an officer in the Norfolk Regiment, Captain Charles Close, gave birth to a healthy girl at about the same time in the same military station and, very soon afterwards, her husband fell gravely ill with enteric fever. In order that the child's crying might not disturb the sleep so necessary to him, Hazel walked up and down the *stoep* (verandah) that surrounded the house in great anxiety and agony of mind for hours at a time. Though she, her husband and their baby returned safely to England, subsequent occupiers of the house saw, on several occasions, the figure of a woman with a baby in her arms, walking backwards and forwards, backwards and forwards, up and down the *stoep*.

A seventeen-year-old girl in India assisted the doctor as midwife to her mother. Subduing her own grief, she broke the news to her mother that the new baby would never see its father, who died suddenly on the march two days earlier.

The Birch sisters, two pretty girls in their teens, were worshipped

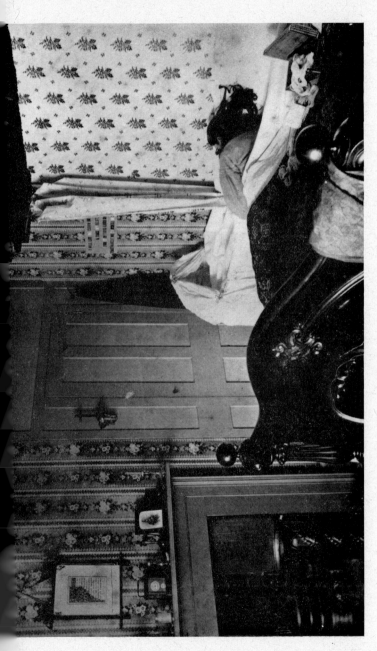

12. An unconventional photograph by Henry Wood, showing his second wife Helen asleep in bed after the birth of their first daughter in a rented house in Southsea

in the Residency Hospital, Lucknow. They nursed the wounded and comforted the dying, battling against festering wounds, flies, total absence of disinfectants and anaesthetics (brandy was given before an amputation) and with smallpox and cholera for good measure.

These women earned no medals, though heaven knows they all deserved them. Emily Polehampton is remembered as a mutiny heroine on her memorial in St. Chad's Church, Shrewsbury. (She married Sir Henry Durand and the tablet is immediately on the right of entry to the main body of the church.) One lady who was awarded a medal, though unofficially, was Mrs. Webber-Harris, wife of Colonel Webber-Harris, 104th Bengal Fusiliers. She was convalescing from a severe bout of Peshawar Fever in the cool of a hill station, when news reached her that cholera had broken out in Peshawar where her husband had remained with the regiment. She immediately decided to return. "Finding that Captain Corbyn was going down the hill, I asked him to take me with him and wired my husband to meet me." Here is a very early use of a well-known army expression. Going "up" or "down" the hill described, in considerable understatement, the annual migration from the hot weather heat of the plains to the cool of 5000 and more feet and back again, a journey that could take several days; and the transport of all household possessions. Civilians went "up to the hills" or "into the *mofussil*" (provinces) and nobody in India ever referred to summer or winter as anything but the hot or cold weather.

Arrived in Peshawar, Mrs. Webber-Harris was aware that her husband, anxious about her health, was vexed with her for joining him. But his annoyance could not hide the sense of relief he felt at having her with him. The epidemic was so virulent, even in its initial stages, that the regiment was ordered to leave Peshawar for an outlying cholera camp at one hour's notice. These camps were the only precaution that could be taken against the spread of the disease and many a lonely cemetery testifies to how ineffectual these precautions proved. Mrs. Webber-Harris accompanied the regiment on their difficult march across country, avoiding the road in case they left "any trail of infection" on the road. Considered in its full implications, this was a horribly necessary measure. Cholera is a hideous disease, which attacks the bowels, causing them to empty painfully and uncontrollably. Several men died on the march from Peshawar and were carried into camp by their living comrades. On arrival, tents were rapidly pitched, and as Mrs. Webber-Harris entered hers, a man seized with cholera collapsed at its door.

The scene that followed is not, in spite of the horror, without the element of comic compromise which so often attended the situation in which the army wife found herself. A doctor arrived and ordered a mustard plaster. "Happily", wrote Mrs. Webber-Harris, "the *khitmatghar* had mustard". Now that *khitmatghars* no longer serve the British families of the army, let that brief understatement be their tribute from generations of sahibs and memsahibs, who could rely on them to produce heaven knows what from heaven knows where in circumstances which would leave a white servant standing. Mrs. Webber-Harris, who had had no time to unpack, tore her handkerchief in half to make the plaster.

During that first night in camp, 27 men died, their deaths necessarily followed by immediate burial in nearby ground. The weather was intensely hot and morale correspondingly low. Colonel Webber-Harris knew that the soldiers' spirits could generally be lifted by singing and organised an impromptu concert, to include a singing competition with prizes—1st Prize, 50 rupees, 2nd Prize, 30 rupees, and so on, ten prizes in all. The men made a gallant attempt at cheerfulness, but flagged before long, "so my husband stepped into the middle and gave them 'Oh had you ever a cousin Tom' which lifted their spirits so that they all shouted with delight and said he should deserve the first prize". Mrs. Webber-Harris gave away the prizes and the men pressed so close round her that her husband, mindful of the risk of infection, took the bag of rupees and began to distribute them himself. But to the men, this was not the same thing at all. One actually refused to accept his prize, putting his hands behind his back and imploring, "Please, let the lady give it to me, sir". Ghostly voices echo from the Crimea, begging for "a touch of your ladyship's hand", voices of men afraid as these were afraid, longing as these longed for the comfort of a woman's touch. Between the beginning of this short prizegiving and its end, the tenth winner had sickened and died.

Both the Webber-Harrises escaped the cholera and when the

epidemic was over, set out exhausted to take some much-needed leave in the hills. The Colonel had to abandon his horse for a string bed, owing to the sudden onslaught of an attack of gout, and they travelled slowly and uncomfortably on, Mrs. Webber-Harris riding some way behind the bearers who carried her husband to keep out of the dust. When it got dark, she sent the *syce*, who walked beside her with a lantern, ahead to give extra light for the coolies carrying the Colonel. So she was quite alone when two men rode up and laid hold of her bridle and the horse's mane. "Feeling frightened, I shouted at the top of my voice", she recounts laconically. Luckily a mounted *sowar* (Indian cavalryman) heard her and galloped back, scaring the men who disappeared. The *sowar* ventured to scold the Colonel's memsahib for riding alone. "This was on the edge of enemy's country and we afterwards lost three camp followers who were murdered by wild hill men." When the Webber-Harrises were finally reunited with the regiment in Peshawar, "I was treated as a heroine, as I had not seen another woman's face for all those three months. Soon afterwards, we heard that the officers had sent home for a gold ornament for me, which proved to be a gold VC, with an inscription 'Presented to Mrs. Webber-Harris by the officers of the Bengal Fusiliers for indomitable pluck during the cholera epidemic of 1869.' General Sir Samuel Brown, himself a VC, asked to be allowed to come to an informal meeting at our own house, when he presented it to me in the presence of the officers, saying he had but one regret, that they had not ordered 'For Pluck' to be put in diamonds on the ribbon."

Commissioned personnel were added to the Army Medical Staff Corps in 1873, and its present title bestowed in 1898. The Army Nursing Service rendered such magnificent service during the Boer War that it was enlarged into Queen Alexandra's Imperial Military Nursing Service, and so continues today as Queen Alexandra's Royal Army Nursing Corps. These reorganisations and reforms naturally affected care of the army family for the better. There were women' wards in most military hospitals by the first decade of this century and, in depot towns, the families were looked after by the regimenta doctor. This was not an entirely satisfactory arrangement, as th doctor in question was not infrequently a retired man who did not reckon on a lot of hard work. One such, who held his appointment for many years, made it clear from the start that he knew nothing at all about obstetrics and would take no responsibility for the care of pregnant women, or the delivery of their offspring. The Louise Margaret, Aldershot, has always been the most famous maternity hospital for the wives of the army.

An insurance scheme for financial help in cases of illness was pioneered by the wife of Sir Malcolm Grover in 1911. Worried about the "stress, anxiety and hardship suffered by families of officers serving in India", she launched the fund subsequently named after her. "At that time", states the fiftieth annual report of the Fund, "there was no provision for free medical care by the government and even medical care by unit medical officers was a secondary duty, only afforded as a privilege. If the patient had to be sent home for treatment, financial embarrassment often added materially to the distress." It did indeed. Amoebic dysentery and sprue often proved fatal if the sufferer remained in India and the inoculations against the dreaded rabies could only be given in London or Paris. In 1912, the title "Lady Grover's Hospital Fund for Officers' Families" was adopted, as a memorial to the foundress, whose premature death occurred that year. In 1923, membership was opened to officers of all three services in any part of the world.

During Captain Sherwood's term of service in India (in the 1840s), women and children, his wife tells us, were admitted to be nursed in the men's wards if there were beds available, but it was subsequently conceded that it was necessary to have purpose-built hospitals, or at least wards. These, though good on the whole, lacked certain home comforts. In one hill station in India, 100 years after the Sherwoods, the journey from the Families' Hospital to the main building, in which the operating theatre was situated, could only be accomplished by ambulance, which had to negotiate a series of hairpin bends and a good deal of up and down hill. Typhoid and meningitis nursed in the same children's ward may have been more distressing for visitors than dangerous to the other patients, but the introduction of a severely mentally-disturbed woman of enormous size, who had attacked a child with a knife and was waiting admission to a mental hospital several hundred miles away, did little for the convalescence of three post-hysterectomy ladies.

On a frosty evening, one woman sat on the edge of her bed in a ward bare of curtains or any kind of covering for the concrete floor, and of which she was the only occupant, waiting for her labour pains to reach the stage when she could be taken to the labour ward. Her plight was nobody's fault. It was simply that the hospital, a small one-storey building in an Indian hill-station, had been officially closed for the winter. All furnishings had been checked and returned to store and an Anglo-Indian nurse had been left in charge till the sergeant's wife, who for medical reasons was not allowed to travel till after the birth of the baby, was delivered and on her feet again. The nurse, while very sorry for her patient, stressed the fact that she had no authority and could not even indent for wood to light a fire.

There was quite a stir when Henry Wood's granddaughter was cured of an internal infection by her Mahomedan bearer. "If memsahib will do what I tell, I will make her better" promised Mahomed Yusef. After several weeks in and out of hospital, with "not yet diagnosed" as the only result of investigations, the patient would, if she had known about him then, have agreed with irreverent Johnny Kincaid in his reflection during the Peninsular War that "some of our people get professionally shot while a great many more visited death by the doctor's road". Nevertheless, when Mahomed Yusef returned from the bazaar with a handful of blackish seed in a screw of newspaper, she did wonder if she was jumping with both feet into the frying-pan. Her confidence was in no way restored when he returned some hours later with a glass of what appeared to be frog-spawn and a bowl of stewed apple. He had soaked the seeds in water for the required time and memsahib would eat the result at once followed by the apple. He administered this unpalatable diet for three days, allowing a little soup as an extra, and at the end of that time, she was well. Interested doctors, worried by the failure of other patients to respond to their official treatment, inquired of the bearer as to his. He could give no explanation beyond the simple statement made with a smile and shrug, "it is what we do in my village".

The health of the army family substantially improved over th years under better conditions of housing and welfare. The dangers attendant on living abroad were reduced by routine vaccination against smallpox and inoculations against typhoid before leaving Britain, followed by subsequent annual boosters. Army "jabs", when every needle had to be indented for and was anything but disposable, could be a painful business, but few mothers, wrestling with a screaming child in a surgery, can have so completely lost their heads as to promise, as one did, "If you aren't a good girl, the doctor won't *ever* inject you again!"

There is no doubt, however, that once it had started the army cared for the health of its families remarkably well, and did so on a scale of charges that would have made any civilian hospital gasp. In 1940, a major's wife had her appendix removed for 50 rupees (£2 10s.), stopped from her husband's pay, while the daily charge for her food was a matter of a few shillings. Past, by more than a century, are the days of spiders crushed and mixed with jam, administered as a medicine to cholera patients. It is to be hoped there can never be a time so heartbreakingly gruelling for the army wife and her children as the siege of Lucknow, where during long hours of burning heat, a woman gave birth to a child in a tiny room, shared with two others suffering from cholera and smallpox respectively.

On July 1st (wrote Emily Polehampton from the Residency), Miss Palmer was wounded in the leg by a round shot, the leg was amputated and no hope seemed to be entertained of her recovery from the first. She was seventeen. Maggie Macdonough, five years younger, walked into the same hospital, saying she had been shot in the head by a bullet. She was able to tell her story with perfect calmness and little thought, poor child, how serious an injury she had sustained. It was necessary to perform a painful operation and to remove a portion of the skull in order to extract it. For a time, she appeared to be going on well, but in less than a fortnight was seized with fits, her whole body becoming paralysed, and sank rapidly. She was a beautiful child and one of Henry's special favourites. Poor Mrs. Macdonough, after her child's death, made herself most useful in attending upon the sick and wounded.

Remarkably, Emily herself remained healthy during the whole

siege, in spite of the fact that she had borne and lost her child only three months before the fighting began. If ever there was a case of hard work being the best medicine, that case was gentle Emmie.

Lady Inglis, wife of Brigadier Inglis, commander of the Residency garrison during the 87 days of the siege, was also aware of the therapeutic value of hard work. "I paid a visit to Mrs. Cowper this evening and did my best to cheer her. She was confined to her bed, most trying at such a time when active employment was the only means to keep one's mind at rest and prevent brooding. I found the children my greatest comfort, as with them to amuse and look after, I never had an idle moment."

Through so many of the letters and diaries of these nineteenth-century women runs the communal theme of faith and trust in the goodness of God. No matter that this was brought about by the pre-vailing climate of the day, or that it went hand-in-hand with other Victorian characteristics not so pleasant; no matter that God was, of course, a white man, or that females were, for the most part, badly educated and therefore brainwashed into believing what they were told. From the depths of sickness, danger, death and bitter woe, they called again and again on the God who would one day welcome them in that "happy land far far away". The Lord giveth, the Lord taketh away, blessed be the name of the Lord. And they meant it.

By the time the bells rang out the old year and the twentieth cen-tury had dawned, the army wife, provided she was on the strength, had begun to lead a life of far greater security than any of her civilian sisters. Her husband was sure of his job up to the moment of his retirement, with pay rises as he himself rose in rank. She was free from the often terrible anxiety of how to raise the few shillings to pay for a visit from the panel doctor. No soup queue, no hard times, no traumatic means test, no dole. It must be owned that the attitude of the officer's wife to her sisters of inferior rank did smack of con-descension and jelly and buns to the poor, but on the whole, the relationship was a good one. So the CO's wife was an old cow? All right, but she was grand that time the baby nearly died in Shanghai and she sat up with it and you all night. Corporal X's wife was a slut, but you had soldiered half the world over together and every time one of you got pregnant, so did the other. It was rather like being married when you come to think of it: soldiering on with the same people, bound together by bonds deeper than friendship "for better, for worse, for richer, for poorer, in sickness and in health" till retirement or death broke the pattern.

References to Chapter 7

Following the Drum, Sir J. W. Fortescue, Blackwood, 1931
Queen Alexandra, G. Battiscombe, Constable, 1969
The Siege of Lucknow, Lady Inglis, Osgood McIlvaine, 1892

Diary of Mrs. Sherwood, Mrs. Sherwood, Houlston
A Memoir, Letters and Diary of the Rev. Henry Polehampton, Richard Bentley, 1858

8. Pictures, Words and Music

SINCE SHAKESPEARE HAS the edge on other writers, it is not surprising that what is probably the earliest literary reference to a British army wife occurs in his play *Henry V*. Agincourt is done and won and the soldiers are hanging about waiting to go home, bored and argumentative. Pistol, the Englishman, scraps with the teasing little Welshman, Fluellen, who insists he eats a leek, even though "Saint Davy's day is past". Then, finding himself alone, Pistol grieves over some news he has lately heard, news that ". . . my Nell is dead i' the spital Of malady of France . . . Old I do wax . . .". What is there to go home for? Life has lost its savour. But not for long. ". . . patches will I get unto these cudgell'd scars, And swear I got them in the Gallia wars". He cheers up, planning his next fiddle.

Three reigns after Gloriana, Robert Farquhar led army wives and girl-friends on stage to make their bow in his rollicking Restoration comedy "The Recruiting Officer". At the end of a plot with as many twists and turns as ever the Severn made round Shrewsbury, Captain Plume marries his Shropshire bride and ends the play pronouncing the laudable sentiment, "And so at home I'll stay And raise recruits the matrimonial way".

Farquhar was not the only Shropshire writer to tell stories of the army. Mrs. Sherwood, already a famous author in 1817, was an officer's wife, and she like Farquhar drew on personal observation and experience, though for very different reasons. There is nothing rumbustious about Mrs. Sherwood's characters. They are either very bad and come to a sticky end, or dreadfully good and expire with pious platitudes and Christian conversions to their credit. The most famous of all her books, *Little Henry and his Bearer*, was still going strong as a Sunday School prize 50 years later, while another so-called work of fiction, *Stories Explanatory of the Church Catechism*, draws a picture not only of little Mary and her pious godmother, the wife of Sergeant Brown, but also gives a graphic account of the tough, often savage life in married quarters in India.

The wife of another paymaster became a widely-read author of books for young people. Julia Horatia Gatty married Major Ewing in 1867 and went as a bride to New Brunswick. She had always been the family story-teller and *Aunt Judy's Magazine* in which many of her works were published took its name from this fact. Her books, *The Peace Egg*, *Lob Lie by the Fire*, *Jackanapes* and *The Story of a Short Life* were published by Bell and Sons for the Society for the Promotion of Christian Knowledge and ran to many editions. Like Mrs. Sherwood, Mrs. Ewing drew on her own experience though she does not appear to have seen such a tough side of army life. It would seem, however, that she had witnessed the building of a military station, which, in *The Story of a Short Life*, she called "Asholt".

Take a Highwayman's Heath (begins Chapter 2), destroy every vestige of life with fire and axe, from the pine that has longest been a landmark, to the smallest beetle smothered in the smoking grass. Burn acres of purple and pink heather and pare away the young bracken that springs verdant from its ashes. Let flames consume the perfumed gorse in all its glory and not spare the broom, whose more exquisite yellow atones for its lack of fragrance. In this common ruin let every lesser flower be involved: blue beds of speedwell by the wayfarer's path—the daintier milkwort and rougher red rattle—down to the very dodder that clasps the heather, let them perish, and the face of Dame Nature be utterly blackened! Then have the heath as bare as the back of your hand and if you have felled every tree, and left not so much as a tussock of grass or a scarlet toadstool to break the force of the winds; then shall the winds come, from the east, from the west, from the north and from the south and shall raise on your shaven heath clouds of sand that would not discredit a desert in the heart of Africa. By some such recipe the ground was prepared for that Camp of Instruction at Asholt which was a thorn in the side of at least one of the neighbours. Then a due portion of this sandy oasis in a wilderness of beauty was mapped out into lines with military precision, and on these were built rows of little wooden huts, which were painted a neat and useful black. The huts for married men and officers were of varying degrees of comfort and homeliness, but those for single men were like toy boxes of wooden soldiers; it was only by doing it very tidily that you could (so to speak) put your pretty soldiers away at night when you had done playing with them, and get the lid to shut down.

Mrs. Ewing made an observation which is not found in other accounts of military quarters. "The low doors to these quarters might be regarded as a practical joke on the part of the authorities, who demand their soldiers shall be both tall and upright, but that man, whether military or not, is an adaptable animal and can get used to anything." She was aware that Asholt and like places would one day be superseded by permanent brick-built camps and garrisons and paid touching tribute to the old garrisons.

> Bare and dusty are the parade grounds, but they are thick with memories. Here were blessed the colours that became a young man's shroud that they might not become a nation's shame. Here march and music welcome the coming and speed the parting regiments. On this parade the rising sun is greeted with gunfire and trumpet clarions shriller than the cock, and there he sets to a like salute with tuck of drum. Here the young recruit drills, the warrior puts on medals, the old pensioner steals back to watch them and the soldiers' children play.

The soldier's child in this book is a little blind boy, but the hero is the rich, beautiful child of the local squire crippled in an accident while watching a military parade, who dies to the strains of "The Son of God goes forth to war" heard through the barrack hut in which he lies.

Another favourite among prizes for good behaviour at school was the edifying *Teddy's Button*, written for the Religious Tract Society by an anonymous author. Teddy, orphaned by some unspecified campaign (the Boer War to judge from the illustrations) is, like Little Henry, an ardent evangelist. Like his predecessor too he makes his principal conversion from a bed of sickness, though, being of a more robust constitution, he does not succumb.

Stories of two children, both very different from Little Henry and Teddy, are told by Kipling and Saki. The subject in each case is the suffering endured at the hands of unkind guardians in times when the climate of the East was considered fatal to any child over seven years old. Both are almost unbearable to read. Punch, the hapless homesick child in *Baa, Baa, Black Sheep* endures in silence because there is nothing else he can do, till finally rescued just in time by his horrified parents. Conradin, in Saki's *Sredni Vashtar*, coldly plans the killing of the guardian he hates by the ferret whose name gives the title to the terrifying story.

And, of course, high above any other army child anybody else ever wrote about stands Kim, who "Though he was burned black as any native; though he spoke the vernacular by preference, and his mother-tongue in a clipped uncertain sing-song . . . was white". His mother was Annie Shott, who was nursemaid to a colonel's children and married Colour Sergeant Kimball O'Hara, who died of cholera but left a son who can justly claim to be the most famous army child in all literature, brain child of the writer who knew the soldier and his wife in India as nobody else has known them—Rudyard Kipling.

The Courting Of Dinah Shadd is one of the best stories of life in married quarters ever written, and the great and searing *Love o'Women* has a magnificent and moving description of the colonel's lady and Judy O'Grady (Dinah again) riding to meet a returning column, not knowing if their husbands are alive or killed.

There are great characters among these soldiers' wives portrayed by Kipling. There is Dinah, "her hair—a winkin' glory over her forehead, big blue eyes beneath, twinkling like stars on a frosty night, and the tread of her two feet lighter than waste paper from the Colonel's basket in the Ord'ly Room". Dinah, whose marriage and motherhood were cursed by Mother Sheehy before ever Terance Mulvaney took her to the altar, "the strong, the patient, the infinitely tender" in the Kipling stories. But even Dinah grew weather-beaten and fat like the "shapeless woman on a pile of bedding loaded on to an army cart" and travelling with the Mavericks.

A rough, tough lot as a whole, who lived, loved and died with their men, like Old Mother Pummeloe, so-called because her shape exactly resembled the fruit of that name. Or they cared for them in sickness and health like Mrs. Bantem, in a story by an anonymous and forgotten author. The wife of Joe Bantem "stood five feet eleven in her socks. She'd got a face nearly as dark as a black's; she'd got a moustache and a good one too; and a great coarse look about her altogether. Joe was as proud of that woman as she was of him; and if anyone hinted about her looks, he used to laugh and say that was only the outside rind and talk about the juice." The men of Joe's company were lucky that she cooked for them "the very best of cooking; not boiled tag and rag, but nice stews and roasts and hashes, when other men were growling over a dog's meat dinner". She saw that they had "the sweetest of clean sheets and never a button off. Our stockings were darned and only let one of us", says Corporal Smith who tells the story, "only let one of us take a drop more than he ought, and see how she'd drop on him, that's all. The long and short of it is Mrs. Bantem was a good motherly woman of forty. She only had one fault and that was she never had any little Bantems to make wives for honest soldiers to come." Mrs. Bantem had her own ideas on this. "I never had any children, and I never wished for any", she said. "They're not right for soldiers' wives. It's what I always did say, soldiers' wives have no business to have children, and it's rank cruelty to bring them into the world."

The Indian Mutiny has inspired many stories and novels, and continues to do so. The most famous in its day was *On the Face of the Waters* by Flora Annie Steel (see p. 124). The little girl who had burnt the effigy of the Nana had long been the wife of an Indian civil servant when her book was first published in 1896, running into many editions. In the preface to this long, sometimes tedious, stupendous and, alas, forgotten novel, the writer states

> I have not allowed fiction to interfere with fact in the slightest degree, nor have I allowed the actual actors in the great tragedy to say a word regarding it which is not to be found in the accounts of eye witnesses or in their own writings. Regarding my fiction. An Englishwoman WAS concealed in Delhi, in the house of an Afghan, and succeeded in escaping to the Ridge just before the siege. I have imagined another; that is all.

The woman thus concealed was an army wife. Among the letters Mrs. Steel received on its publication was one which read, "My wife died in the Mutiny. After forty years, you have taught me to forgive".

Another very popular novel of 50 years ago was *Captain Desmond VC* by Maud Diver, granddaughter of Sir Henry Lawrence. In this, the army wife is badly served. A silly, frivolous creature of no account, married to the inhumanly honourable hero, she has to be disposed of to make room for the sister of his brother officer, who has clear eyes, wonderful hair, a character to match, and who nobly conceals her love for Desmond. Sisters often seem to have been of this calibre and the devotion between them and their soldier brothers could almost be said to smack of the Byronic. Family relationships would seem to have changed slightly over the years, if a conversation between a subaltern home on leave from India, and his pater and mater is anything to go by:

Pater: I suppose you'll be turning up some fine day with a girl under your arm, if you haven't got one now, eh?
Subaltern: You can make your mind easy, sir. I haven't one.
Mater: Not in all these years?
Subaltern: I hadn't time, mummy. They keep a man pretty busy these days in the service, and most of our Mess are unmarried too.

Another subaltern dying of cholera hears some strains of music and the Surgeon Major bends to catch his last words, "Not that waltz. That's our own, our very ownest own, Mummy dear".

Since these embarrassing extracts come from the pen of the creator of Mowgli, Kim, Mulvaney and Mrs. Hawksbee, it can only be presumed that people really did talk like that. Sugar-coated mothers and golden-haired lisping tots are among the less believable and certainly less likeable of all the characters in soldier-literature. War, the army and the British Raj are dirty words and all continue to fascinate writers and the reading public. Paul Scott, in a magnificent sequence, paints a truly representative picture of the last days of the Raj and the army in India, and Manohar Malgonkar, with *The Devil's Wind*, gives the first reasoned account of one phase of the Mutiny from the Indian point of view.

Nor has the soldier and his family been neglected by artists. True, the family have no part in the huge battle scenes painted by Lady Butler (herself an officer's wife and mother) and other heroic scenes that adorn messes and drill halls. For generations, however, children in their schoolrooms wondered what answer the long-haired boy in blue satin would give to the question rapped out by the Puritan colonel, "When did you last see your father?". The original painting by W. F. Yeames hangs in the Liverpool Art Gallery and was associated in many a child's mind with an equally popular book *The Children of the New Forest* by Marryat. In "The Order of Release", Millais is said to have painted a picture with a double meaning, since the model for the young woman in the picture was the wife of Ruskin whom Millais loved and subsequently married. George Morland also included a "Deserter Pardoned" among his series of paintings of army recruits, and both Rowlandson and Singleton painted the family at home and on the move. Sir Noel Paton's "Return From The Crimea" is one of the very finest of this sort of picture, the figures splendid, the detail ravishing.

The Indian Mutiny was a much-painted event. "Jessie's Dream" (an entirely fictional incident) by F. Goodall hung on the walls of manor and cottage alike, and there are large impressive paintings of the happenings at Delhi, Lucknow and Cawnpore. All these were studio works, bearing little relation to the circumstances of the actual occurrences. Among the hundreds of water-colour records of army life (Captain Corbett's and Colonel Wood's among them), the mild treatment of the scene inside the Massacre House at Cawnpore by a young officer who painted what he saw is, in its very gentleness, truly terrible. There were many charming subjects too. Colonel Palmer and his Indian wife posed for Zoffany, Chinnery recorded the graceful Larkins children, Lady George Paget sits in her Scutari drawing-room, and tucked away in a family album is a self-portrait of Henry Wood's daughter, Olive, aged six.

With the Crimean War, photography took over. One picture shows a solemn, well-dressed child seated on a gun, surrounded by a group of officers and one civilian, with Ensign Henry Wood seated and reading a book in the foreground. Roger Fenton, the best-known of the photographers officially sent out to record the campaign, took pictures of ladies and wives, as well as battlefields, including Fanny Duberley on Bob.

Of the numbers of songs which tell of the soldiers' life and loves one of the best known was "Brighton Camp". Under its other title of "The Girl I Left Behind Me", it must have caused many a tear and

3. Photograph by Ensign Henry Wood (seated on the ground, reading), in which a small boy sits on a gun captured in the Crimea

not a few sighs of relief as regiments marched away to its merry tune. "The Captain with the Whiskers" twirled them to good effect wherever he went, while "Polly Oliver" dressed herself up in her dead brother's clothes and went for a soldier to follow her love. It is to be hoped she had more luck than the girl who kept on imploring "Soldier, Soldier, Will You Marry Me", only to discover at the end of a great many verses that he had a wife at home.

Wars always occasion songs, written for, but not by, soldiers. A good tune shouted at the top of the voice helps a man to forget hunger and blisters, but the fighting man is not often a poet or musician and seldom gets round to doing more than fit ribald words to tunes learnt in Sunday School. "When the Bloody War is Over" sung to the rousing tune of "What a Friend We Have in Jesus", meant no blasphemy on the part of those who sang. The words were their own and came from the heart, while the tune was part of childhood and home. "The Church's One Foundation" fitted a song about the army and the Royal Flying Corps combined, which included a meeting with the Kaiser who exclaimed "Hoch hoch mein Gott, what a bloody fine lot".

But for the most part, the songs the soldier sang were written far from any battlefield and popularised via the music hall. From the Boer War have survived "Bring the Flag Back to Majuba", "Bring My Daddy Home Again" and the immortal "Dolly Gray". 1914–18 were the great singing years of the army. "Mademoiselle from Armentières" with its "inky pinky parley vou" was more for the concert party entertaining troops at the Front than for the drawing-room, but "Keep the Home Fires Burning" by the young Ivo Novello sounded as well to piano accompaniment as belted out on the march. "Tipperary" was sung and whistled by everybody, from the army to the children in the nursery and the butcher boy on his bike. "On Monday I Go out With a Soldier, On Tuesday With a Tar" expressed from behind the footlights the admiration of the singer for those who were "doing their bit" in uniform and who might be in danger of getting killed, but not of receiving the white feather.

One song only is couched in officer-terminology. The silly touching

> Bonsoir old thing
> Cheerio chin chin
> Napoo toodleoo
> Goodbyeeeeeee

could only be part of the nonchalance of the subaltern. And when the bloody war was finally over, the young burst into song with the equally silly, infectious "K-K-K-Katie, beautiful Katie, You're the only g-g-g-girl that I adore".

Nobody, it seems, has so far written an opera or even an operetta about the British army wife or daughter, which is a pity since there are two such heroines from other countries. "Madame Sans Gêne" tells the story of the washerwoman who becomes the wife of one of Napoleon's generals, and Donizetti in "The Daughter of the Regiment" takes a Swiss orphan, gives her a happy childhood round camp fires, proves her to be the daughter of a high-born lady and sees her suitably married off. Rudyard Kipling uses the same title and in a commendably concise story gets Jhansi McKenna (sister to Muttra, Colaba and "a whole presidency of other McKennas") wedded to Corporal Slane.

Nor do the army wife or daughter appear to have inspired great poetry. The seventeenth-century Richard Lovelace expresses regret to his Lucasta (tinged with slight relief?) that he must leave her to go to the wars, justifying himself by the well-worn excuse: "I could not love thee Dear so much Loved I not honour more".

Jessie makes her appearance again in a poem by Whittier: "Dinna ye hear it? Dinna ye hear it? The pipes o' Havelock sound", she implores, as the relieving force approaches.

But sometimes tragedy is expressed with a poem of great dignity and beauty as in "The Bridegroom", by Rudyard Kipling.

> Call me not false beloved
> If, from thy scarce known breast
> So little time removed
> In other arms I rest
>
> For this more ancient bride
> Whom coldly I embrace
> Was constant at my side
> Before I saw thy face

Our marriage often set
By miracle delayed
At last is consummate
And cannot be unmade

Live then, whom life shall cure
Almost, of memory
And leave us to endure
Its immortality.

This says what many a soldier and his wife have inarticulately felt in time of war.

"The Ballad of Reading Gaol" was dedicated by Oscar Wilde to Trooper Wooldridge, Royal Horse Guards, hanged on July 7th, 1896, for the murder of his pretty, well-brought-up young wife after a jealous quarrel. Wilde, who never met Wooldridge, watched him exercising in the prison yard, remembering afterwards that:

He did not wear his scarlet coat
For blood and wine are red
And blood and wine were on his hands
When they found him with the dead,
The poor dead woman whom he loved
And murdered in her bed.

But Kipling's soldiers (with the exception of Mulvaney and Larry Tighe) are not usually introspective, nor their wives either. He knew what we were like and he wrote it down in verse:

What did the colonel's lady think?
Nobody ever knew
Somebody asked the sergeant's wife
And she told them true
When you get to the man in the case
They're as like as a row of pins
For the colonel's lady and Judy O'Grady
Are sisters under their skins.

References to Chapter 8

Captain Desmond, *VC*, Maud Diver
Children of the New Forest, F. Marryat, Collins, 1954
The Devil's Wind, Mahonat Malgonkar
Jackanapes, J. H. Ewing, Bell & Sons for the Society for the Promotion of
    Christian Knowledge
Kim, R. Kipling, Macmillan, 1908
Little Henry and his Bearer, Mrs. Sherwood, Houlston
Lob Lie by the Fire, J. H. Ewing, Ball & Sons for the S.P.C.K.
Lucy and her Dhaye, Mrs. Sherwood, Houlston, 1817
Mascots of the Services, Major T. J. Edwards, Gale & Polden, 1953
On the Face of the Waters, F. A. Steel
The Peace Egg, J. H. Ewing, Bell & Sons for the S.P.C.K.
Stories Explanatory of the Church Catechism, Mrs. Sherwood, Houlston,
    1817
The Story of a Short Life, J. H. Ewing, Bell & Sons for the S.P.C.K.
Teddy's Button, Anon., Religious Tract Society
This Happy Breed, R. Hargreaves, Skeffington, 1951
Tommy Atkin's Children, Col. St. John Williams, H.M.S.O., 1971
Works by Kipling
Works by Saki

9. *Children and Animals*

ARMY CHILDREN ARE born into a fantastic inheritance. Their very names have sometimes marked them as creatures apart. A son born to the wife of Sergeant Major Allcock on board the troopship *Aboukir* was named after the vessel. Worse was to befall a girl infant born on the *Shooting Star* during the Crimean War and given the unmanageable name of "Euxenia". Her father, a private soldier, was unlikely to have known that Euxine was the ancient name for the Black Sea, and my guess is that a young officer with classical pretensions persuaded the parents to load the child with what must have been a millstone round her neck for life.

A baptismal certificate of 1869 records the names of a child as "Helvetia Mary Malabar". These were bestowed upon her in the name of the Father, the Son and the Holy Ghost after she and her mother had survived the difficult confinement on the *Helvetia*, a horrible old ship adapted for trooping, transferring to the *Malabar* at Port Said for the rest of the voyage to India. It is to be presumed that Mary was inserted on the Christian insistence of clergyman or godparents, and surprising that she was not known by that simple name, with those of the old tubs appearing only on certificates and legal documents. But she left the font as Helvetia and was so-called all her life.

Baptisms on board were common, often from necessity and equally often followed by one, if not two, funerals; but christenings aboard could be joyful and social occasions. When HMS *Nelson* put into Gibraltar for the winter cruise the chaplain gave her name to little Nelsona Robinson. Boys were not infrequently named after military heroes, Napier and Gordon being popular choices, while the Queen and Miss Nightingale cast their illustrious shadow over many a baby girl.

Less frequent were the unfortunates of either sex called after battles, though this did occasionally happen and was attributed in some cases to the Aldershot Military Tattoo. The din of the battle scenes in this splendid annual spectacle kept the population for miles round awake night after night for a week. It also brought on the labour pains of those incautious enough to attend a performance too near their time, and more than one baby is alleged to have been delivered in the first-aid tent. Officers' ladies often had regimental children named after them, but few can have been so complimented as Henry Wood's daughter, Olive. As the wife of the Governor of Bermuda, she did valuable work among poor families, and a grateful young woman, asked to name her child at the font, replied "whatever Lady Cubitt's names are".

Life and death were only too often closely linked in the early days, when the birth took place behind the piece of sacking that screened off the family's living quarters. Any groan or shriek of anguish could disturb the sleep of up to 80 men. If the mother died, her body was carried through the barrack room; if she survived, she and her new-born child lay in the disease-ridden atmosphere for just so long as it took her to struggle to her feet again. Death for mother and child was common—it is only amazing that survival was common too.

Army children certainly enjoyed perks and privileges that never came the way of their civilian contemporaries of whatever social rank. There were welfare clinics in garrison and depot towns, and there were entertainments organised at company or regimental level throughout the year.

Very familiar among these was the Christmas party, the procedure for which followed a strict set of rules. In one regiment, the sum of 6d. per year of every child's age was allowed to be spent on a present, distributed by Father Christmas after an enormous tea laid out in one of the barrack rooms. The officers' wives did the shopping, and a headache it was. Every mother knew precisely what her child/ children were entitled to, exactly what could be bought and where. No economising by taking advantage of a bargain and putting the money saved to any other child's advantage! A shopping list of 30-odd years ago makes interesting reading. Watches from Marks and Spencer at 5s. (the top price of any goods sold in these stores at that time) kept every ten-year-old happy till the inevitable fatal over-winding. Doll's prams on the other hand presented an insuperable problem. They too could be bought for five shillings, but the six-

12

year-olds, who yearned for them, were not entitled to this amount being spent, and the price to be paid in other shops would be more than could be spent on the child's behalf. As has been already remarked, there was no question of robbing Peter to pay Paul. Dolls and torches, easy to find at about half-a-crown, presented further problems. If Bobby, aged ten, wanted a torch with red and green shutters, back had to go the shopping wives to ask Bobby's mother what he wanted for the remaining half-crown.

A great-grandchild of Henry Wood remembers loathing these parties, feeling herself outside, different, and resentful of being drawn, even temporarily, into a society she didn't know and was afraid of, because her clothes were different and she and her sister arrived by car, accompanied by Nanny. These unrecognised guilt feelings would have surprised her parents very much if she had been able to express them.

Most officers' children had nannies. Proper nannies in print dresses for indoors and grey or navy coats and hats for walking in the afternoon. The richer nannies had a nursery maid as well. Nannies went by the name of "their" family and were often "plus famille que famille". They might boss the soldier servant in a way the mistress would never dare to do, boasting about her employer's promotion, lording it over the nannies of inferior army rank. But the army nanny was a wonderful woman, often paid a good deal less than she could have expected in a civilian household and taking the rough with the smooth at home and abroad.

Of course, she had great fun and a more interesting time than stay-at-home nannies. She was often widely travelled, with a fund of stories and shelves full of souvenirs to be treasured and dusted in retirement, their every detail a delight to her "children's" children when they went to tea with "grandnanny". She rarely took much account of "foreign ways", as she was pleased to call the general ambience of any country other than her own. A nursery was a nursery wherever you were, and British at that. One nanny spent four years in India on just one Hindustani word—*pani* (water). Not *garm* (hot), or *tunda* (cold), or *gussell* (bath), or drinking or any other kind of *pani*! Just *pani*, and a household of servants knew just what she meant.

This attitude produced a marvellous security for the children. In the social merry-go-round of foreign army stations, nanny was often a far more stable figure than their parents. She had invitations to dances and concerts and to other entertainments. Indeed, she often found a husband, whom she married after a courtship followed with fascinated interest by her charges, who would cry bitterly when she left and often followed her up the aisle as bridesmaids.

One nanny gave her life for "her" family, the Grissell children, Henry's Wood's grandchildren. Their father, Colonel Bernard Grissell, the Norfolk Regiment, was reported missing in April 1917, his death not being established till six months later. Olive Grissell was left with four children, ranging in age from nine to one year. Their much-loved nanny was Rose Starkey, a plump bright-eyed girl from a village near Norwich. Her young man was allowed to visit the nursery and then she married him because he was going to the Front. This mysterious word had terror for the eldest child. She could not imagine where it could possibly be, but dreadful things happened there. She was horrified on a seaside visit to be told they were "going for a good blow on the Front". Nanny's husband was sent home from France, badly gassed, in the winter of 1918, at the beginning of the fearful influenza epidemic. She was requested, along with many other relatives, to go, if possible, to the hospital and nurse him, as the staff was decimated by the virus. She took the train to Whitchurch in Shropshire, the nearest station to Prees Heath Hospital. Every day until her husband's death, she made her way, often on foot, from her lodgings in Whitchurch to the hospital several miles away. There, she did a day's heavy duty and went back again.

As a 22-year-old widow, she packed her bag and returned to the Grissells to find that they too had all contracted influenza. She, and a wonderful parlourmaid named Randall, nursed the whole family for at least two weeks. Olive Grissell, perforce the first to recover, got up from her bed as nanny, too late, was obliged to give in and take to hers. Two of the convalescent children were sent away to friends and of the others left behind, Rosemary, seven years old, lay awake in the frightening dark, listening to the unexplained sounds of nanny dying. The news, when broken to the children, meant more to them than the death of their father, happy memories of whom were fading into the background where they would remain in that sunlit happiness so many childhood memories seem to have. Though one of them never forgot the telegram delivered on a sunlit evening, the bad news it brought was far away, while this was near, immediate and terrible.

Flinging herself on her mother in bitter grief, the ten-year-old Veronica groped desperately for some sort of consolation, something definite that could be done to take at least part of the hurt away. In the back of her mind was talk she had heard about a grave to be made for an unknown soldier so that, as her mother had explained, daddy and everyone else who had lost their lives could be honoured. Choking and crying, she blurted out "and nanny ought to be buried in Westminster Abbey". Veronica, a voracious reader with a strong predilection for the macabre, decided during her convalescence to write a short story. "The body lay on its bier," she wrote, "surrounded by corpse candles." Though she had no very clear idea, then or now, what corpse candles actually were, and though the story never got further off the ground than that opening sentence, she still considers it her best punch line.

An early memory for any army child was the Sunday Church Parade. This always took place after Morning Service in any garrison town at home or abroad. Religion played an important part in the lives of many soldiers who were great Christians, but it is true to say that in its outward forms, army religion was a thing on its own. Church Parade was compulsory, so the church was always full. The General Officer commanding the district or division read one, if not both, lessons. Olive Wood's second husband was a distinguished soldier, Major General Sir Thomas Astley Cubitt, who, splendid in medals and red tabs, glared over his family in the front pew and addressed the congregation with the terse remark "I'll give you half a minute to get the coughing over", before exhorting them to put Uriah the Hittite in the front of the battle or thundering through the story of David and Goliath. Sir Thomas, despite a tremendous reputation for violent language, had principles springing from Quaker ancestry, which included a horror of anything he considered Popish. He once embarrassed his wife considerably while attending a service in a strange church where the Creed was intoned. Slamming his fist down on to the pew in front of him, he exclaimed in righteous indignation and at the top of his voice "Damn it, this is most irreverent".

After Church Parade, the General, surrounded by senior officers and his and their wives and families, watched the Parade march off in a powerful smell of hot feet and bootblacking, brasso, pipe clay and sweat.

Up and down the country, many countries, the army children travelled by horse-drawn wagon and steam train, and even camels, the household goods and clothes and treasures expertly packed by women who knew exactly how to do the job from long practice and who lost singularly little by breakage.

And there was India, the special India of the British Raj, where every Baba was a king and to which these kings and queens went generation after generation to rule their kingdoms for the brief few years that seemed to them a lifetime. Their subjects were the servants, pet dogs and ponies, the monkeys and minah birds, the Rikki Tikki mongoose and the green parrots that flew shrieking from tree to tree. Their enemies were the climate, the snake and the rabid dog. None of this must be confused with the adult India, to which it bore little resemblance and with which it had even less relation. Though the Indian Mutiny was a volcanic eruption, the lava of which spread and corroded far and wide, it did not, once it was over, affect the lives of children. The early illustrations to the stories of Mrs. Sherwood show rooms little different to those occupied by Hazel and Olive Wood nearly 50 years later. In photographs, Freddy and Cecil Wood pose on the bungalow verandah, surrounded by their toys. Olive and Hazel play cooking just as Olive's children and grandchildren did in their later generations.

Children were so loved and protected in India that they felt safe to a greater degree than they would probably feel for the rest of their lives. That this safety was an illusion, their parents knew only too well. The evidence of diaries and letters show clearly that bereavement was an everyday part of living, evidence borne out by grandiose monuments in the graveyards in which lie those who died young and far from home.

Mary, beloved wife of Robert, aged twenty. Also Robert her son, aged two days

Susan, Jane and Amelia, the children of Captain and Mrs. X

The most touching of them all is probably the sadly funny grave of Sergeant and Mrs. Rabbit and their many children in Sitapur. Up and down India, the story is told of children who died of cholera, typhoid, dysentery, sunstroke, snakebite, malaria, rabies and tuberculosis. All this is documented and well known, as is every other aspect of the life of the British Raj. There can be no documentation of the world in which the children lived, a world between that of the grown-ups, which they did not understand and so disregarded, and that of the servants, with which they were often familiar to an extent that would have astounded and horrified their parents. In this world, there was no distinction between social rank or profession. The *baba-log* (literally "child people") were there to be waited on, give orders and be thoroughly spoiled, whether they were the children of a general or a private soldier. This turned them into odious little tyrants, as grandparents and other sufferers discovered.

There was a snob value about having a British nanny in India, though the children looked after by ayahs were the ones whose memories later held the richest store. Ayah—a brown-faced woman, with shiny, coal-black hair and rings round her ankles, on her toes and in her nose. She had a round metal box, which she produced from the folds of her white sari when your mother was out, sorting out its mysterious contents from their several compartments and wrapping them up in a green leaf, which she put into her mouth with a special flicking gesture and chewed. Veronica Grissell used to persuade ayah to give her a little piece of this strange concoction. It had an extraordinary taste, but she liked it. Ayah would never allow her to have any of the red mixture she painted on the leaf, as it stained the teeth and the memsahib would have been angry. Bazaar sweets, brightly coloured and forbidden, were another delight her parents never knew about, any more than she was aware 30 years later that her daughter preferred vegetable curry in the servants' godown to the Irish stew of the nursery. Ayah, however good, on the whole did show a certain irresponsibility and had to be constantly watched over boiling milk and drinking water. If she was Muslim, she became irritable from fasting during the period of Ramadan, the date of which varied year by year and which lasted a month. If she was Hindu, there was a faint possibility she might dope her charges with opium or fondle the penis of a boy baby, though these stories are probably a good deal exaggerated.

What has not been exaggerated, in fact is never sufficiently regarded, are the stories of those ayahs and other Indian servants who saved the lives of the babas and, in some cases, the mothers during the Mutiny. One ayah is known to have crept out of the compound with the white child, stained with dye and justifiably drugged with opium, hidden in her sari, leading the mother and two elder children to eventual safety. The feelings of the poor mother must have been indescribable, as the escape had been delayed owing to the necessity of burying the fourth child who had died earlier in the day. The happy ending to this story shows a certain lack of sensitivity. The disguises in which the family made their escape were neither burnt as reminders of events too painful to recall, nor kept as treasured relics, but consigned to the dressing-up box, where they eventually disintegrated from constant use.

In England, the horrors of the sufferings of the British reverberated even in the nurseries. Young Flora Annie Webster, later to write the greatest novel on the subject and the first to recognise that the Indian did not play an utterly villainous part, burnt the Nana Sahib in effigy. Of all the children whose bones are part of Indian dust, none died more horribly than those who perished in that hideous, mysterious episode, and no story of survival is more interesting than that reported by the Commissioner of Meerut:

Amid all the villainies and horrors of which we have been witnesses, some pleasing traits of native character have been brought to light. All the Delhi fugitives have to tell of some acts of protection and rough hospitality. Only yesterday, a faquir came in with a European child he had picked up on the banks of the Jumna—he refused any payment, but expressed the hope that a well might be made to commemorate the act, and Imam Bhartee will, I hope, live long in the memory of man.

Long too in the memory of many men and women will live memories without which they would have been the poorer, had there been no ayah to sing the traditional lullaby: "Go crow, go crow, Ripe plums are two a penny"; to squat on her haunches, a little distance from the sandpits and swings of the children's playground at the Club, that essential part of British life in India, or anywhere else, where all the officers' children played in the afternoon. Nanny, children and ayah children played together; the ayahs would salaam the nannies who sat apart and despised them.

Then, you were seven years old and the time had come for you to go Home. Back to England, out of reach of all the dangerous health hazards, and to school. Such separation could be disastrous to family relationships. Parents and children found themselves at the end with broken contacts that took years to repair, if indeed they ever fully mended at all. It is doubtful if many children were really ill-treated by their guardians. *Baa, Baa, Black Sheep* may have been drawn from Rudyard Kipling's own experience, but Antirosa is no more typical of her kind than Conradin's guardian in Saki's terrible *Sredni Vashtar*. But the fact that these two stories could have been written by two men with personal experience throws the traumatic effect of this unavoidable situation sharply into focus. Unavoidable it was, since up to the Second World War and the development of air travel, the journey to India took three weeks by sea. It is possible, with hindsight, to feel that there may have been an element of hysteria about it all. Children of the Other Ranks, whose parents could not afford to send them home and pay double housekeeping, did not, even in pre-antibiotic days, all meet with early death.

On the contrary any number of them lived to grow up as strong and healthy as any other children anywhere else. There was the annual migration "up the hill" though at least one sergeant's wife declared that her son did much better on the plains in the hot weather and it is certainly a moot point as to whether the possible physical risk of disease and the debilitation thought to be caused by the climate were any worse than the certain risk of the alienation and shyness between parents and children caused by the years of separation.

Education continued both on the plains and in the hills and there was the Lawrence School at Sanawar to which boys could go as boarders. Army children could be born in India and never see England till they were in their teens or over. On leaving school the boys often joined their father's regiment or were, less often, recruited into the Indian Railways. The girls were in great demand as nannies to officers' children. The army young who did not go home or die had a very good time indeed leading lives far gayer than their contemporaries at home could ever hope to do, and, in the case of the girls, marrying much younger.

The guardians of the children in exile in Britain were, for the most part, grandparents, aunts and uncles who absorbed the new-comers into adequately-staffed houses, or country parsons who welcomed the extra money and could offer holiday coaching to supplement a hitherto sketchy education.

That the children were homesick for the life they had left, that they missed their parents and the sun and the colour and sounds among which they had been brought up, was true. It is also true, at any rate for some, that the introduction to a more permanent way of life and the absence of any kind of makeshift caused a certain envy, and a feeling of being in some way what would now be called a second-class citizen. Houses set in parks where ancient trees threw long shadows on endless green, so very different from eucalyptus and pine and mango *topes* (plantations); the squire's children who didn't want to hear about India, and why should they when they had lived in one place so long that their ancestors lay in armour, ruff and farthingale alongside the family pew in church? The children might be dull, and they might say you were bragging because you told them you had been torpedoed coming home and had held your little brother up for two hours in the water, but they were secure—as you had been once. They didn't have to feel guilty because the memory of parents was fading (sometimes you couldn't, in panic, remember exactly what they looked like), and the business of letter-writing became more and more difficult, because in spite of all you were doing there seemed less and less to say.

Guardians in the holidays. In the term-time, school. Several of these catered especially for army children, notably Cheltenham, where many a distinguished soldier has received his education, and the Royal School for Girls at Bath. Founded in 1864 with a public subscription list headed by Her Majesty the Queen, its aim was "to provide for the daughters of the army, at the lowest cost, a thoroughly sound, practical and religious education". These aims remain the same over a century later. This famous school is not the oldest of its kind—that distinction being claimed by Princess Helena's College, founded in 1818 "for the education of the daughters of the clergy of the Church of England and of Naval and Military officers who died for their country in the Napoleonic Wars". Pupils were admitted at the age of eight and remained till they were 21, learning "the manufacture of the spinning of lace, the English language, arithmetic, sacred and profane history and the use of the globes". The green uniform, slightly naval in design, remained regulation for many years. The school has moved twice since its foundation and now flourishes in Hertfordshire.

Years before any of these, the first school to be instituted and maintained entirely for and by the army was started in, of all places, Tangier, which became a British possession and a garrison as part of the dowry of Catherine of Braganza. It is tantalising, if understandable, that nothing is now known about it except the year of its foundation, 1675, and the names and salaries of its two schoolmasters, Richard Reynolds MA and John Eccles, a gunner, who each received £30 p.a.

Army education progressed slowly from this small beginning. In 1770, the Royal Hibernian School in Dublin was the first boarding school to be paid for out of public funds. There were 90 boys and 50 girls, whose extra-curricular activities included gardening, tree-planting and lace-making. Four years later, Sergeant Lamb of the 9th Foot ran a small school in barracks for the children of NCOs. The foundation stone of the most famous of all was laid in 1801 by the "Grand Old Duke of York", then commander-in-chief, and named the "Royal Military Asylum for the children of the soldiers of the Regular Army". Situated in Chelsea, its staff was headed by a chaplain, whose title was "Superintendent of Morals and Education". The establishment was co-educational, and in spite of being strictly superintended, various boys and girls "contrived to elude this vigilance" by scaling a high wall. The girls were moved to

Southampton, where their school did not long survive, and the
boys to Dover, where, as the Duke of York's School, it remains
today.

In 1808, the children of the Rifle Corps were given regimental
schooling and, seven years later, the first school to operate on active
service was established at Lisbon, by order of the Duke of Wellington. His lordship's concern was for the education of his soldiers, but
there were certain gaps in their time for learning and their place was
taken by the raggle-taggle children, rounded up to keep them out of
mischief. A remarkable little school was started in 1816 for the
children of soldiers on active service in Katmandu by an officer on
sick leave, who continued to run it for eight years.

In England, the first regimental school was started by the 1st
Regiment of Guards stationed in the Tower of London in 1762. The
pupils were taught in a room set aside for the purpose, coal and
candles provided, for an overall fee of twopence per week, rather
high in proportion to their fathers' pay.

Following an application from the Royal Cape Mounted Rifle
Corps for a schoolmistress to teach the army children, a Royal
Warrant was issued for the appointment of one schoolmistress for
every regiment.

At Colchester, both boys and girls were taught what would now
be called "domestic science", and in other army schools, girls who
did needlework were allowed to keep the clothes they made "as this
reconciles their mothers to the loss of their daughters' services at
home".

Scotland has its own school for the sons of its regiments,
established in 1903 at Dunblane.

All army schools were regularly inspected and the pupils medi-
cally examined. The doctors' reports, together with those of the
teachers, went with the child from school to school. Army Form
C-319 (Modified for India) states that Teresa Margaret Bamfield
Henry Wood's great-granddaughter) was in a normal state of health,
clean, of average physique and weighed 46 pounds. One teacher
found her intelligent and well behaved and considered she would
make a good scholar, while to another she seemed to be "vaguely
muddling along".

Army schoolmasters and mistresses had a fairly unrewarding job, which they did very well indeed. Their pupils had often been to so many schools that they had lost interest in any kind of learning. Parents were not obliged to send their children to army schools, but they usually did. When they did not, it was not a reflection on the school itself. Occasionally parents like the Bamfields felt it a pity to live in Lucknow and behave as if one was still at Aldershot.

Sending their daughters, Phyllida and Tessa, to the Loretto Convent, whose Superior in 1939 was Mother Mary Charles, earned them raised eyebrows for going slightly native, but it was a happy time for the children. They were at that time the only white pupils, but as the nuns were English or Irish and the teaching entirely in English, this was no problem, and the lessons for seven-year-olds were much what they would have been for a comparable age group at home. The school day, however, was different. They departed by *tum-tum* (a small pony-drawn carriage on two wheels) with seating for two, and the pony boy stood on a small foot platform at the rear. By the time the lunch break arrived, a number of servants were waiting at the gates with their tiffin carriers. These consisted of two or three aluminium containers fitted one on top of the other, the food kept hot by lighted charcoal in a special compartment underneath. When the warm weather started, the hours altered—seven o'clock till midday and no school in the afternoon. By the time the hot weather set in, it was school in the hills for the army children, to which many rode on ponies. On one notable occasion, they were kept indoors nearly all day, not on account of bad behaviour, but because of a plague of locusts, a rarity so high above the plains. The air was darkened by their metallic wings and when the sound and darkness passed, the children rode home through disgusting ruin, the ponies picking their way hoof deep among insects flopped down never to rise again, scrub, oak and pine destroyed and broken.

So many memories the army children have. Train journeys in India always began at night, and could take anything up to two days, "going up the hill" at the beginning of the hot weather, and "going down the hill" at the end of it. These expressions belonged to the

United Provinces, now Uttar Pradesh in Bengal. You went "to the mofussil". Other regions no doubt had their own terms for the bi-annual migrations. It was all exciting and, at moments, alarming. At any and every station all hell broke loose, waking children from sleep, frightened at the noise and the huge shadows distorted against the wire gauze of the windows. But really it was only people selling things, *Hindu char* (tea), *Muslim char*, *chapattis* (unleavened breadcakes), sweetmeats and toys. Bernard Grissell bought his daughters each a perch of bright green *papier mâché* parrots to amuse them on a journey, and there was much else, some of it rubbish, to buy as souvenirs.

The playthings of India had their own magic. Painted clay sets of household servants; lions, tigers, horses and other animals jewel-painted from Benares; tiny brilliant bowls and jugs; a flute of the kind played in the hills in the rainy season, when the wood is favourably conditioned by the damp atmosphere to give lovely haunting notes; an ugly calico doll made by the bearer's wife for missy baba and dressed like a Muslim bride; cresset lamps moulded in clay and begged from the servants after Diwali, the Feast of Lights. There were other lamps placed on a mysterious tomb in the garden which were not to be touched. An Indian soldier killed in the Mutiny, they said.

Nursery food had to be carefully prepared and protected because of the risk of dysentery. All milk was boiled and, consequently, disgusting, but the jug covers were beautiful, rounds of muslin weighted down with blue and yellow beads. Fruit was delicious, oranges, grapes, melon, papaya, but had always to be dipped in pinky pani—a disinfectant made from permanganate of potash—which looked splendidly purple till you spilt it and were scolded for the brown stain.

Shake your slippers before you put them on—there might be a scorpion inside. Don't knock a leech off if you see it on your leg or you won't be able to stop the bleeding. Wait till someone brings some salt to put on and then it will disgustingly wither and drop off. Monkeys were always a nuisance and not only in India, where they are sacred and must not be shot. An officer stationed in Gibraltar complained that they not only appropriated his rocking chair and attacked his children, but stole his trousers. A menace swoops out of the sky in the shape of a shrike hawk and children in a hill station are told never to carry food or anything bright in their hands out of doors. Jackals raced by, their wild shrieks flung behind them. You could stop their noise by putting your slippers, toes touching, facing the direction of the sound, but nothing could stop the blood-curdling yell of the King Jackal shattering the night. A panther's cough could spell danger to any dog sleeping on a verandah even in daylight, and many a child in the strangeness of Home has found it hard to sleep without the nightlight necessary for so long because of snakes. Not all animals were dangerous or malicious. Pets have always been a great feature of army life, distinct from official regimental mascots, which are part of an old, honourable and mysterious tradition. Dogs and cats, parrots, talking mynahs, canaries, a pet lamb, a deer, budgerigars, tortoises—these were among the many that travelled with the soldier and his family.

Of all the pets, those with the least survival-potential were the glow-worms, painstakingly collected every evening and gently placed in cups where they glowed brightly in the dark. But the glow-worms were always dead by morning and had a funny smell. Animals who went to war were sometimes put on the strength, being actually treated better than the wives, as there was no ballot for them and they were entitled to rations. All families in the Peninsular War must have been perfectly familiar with Copenhagen, the famous horse on which the Duke of Wellington rode to hounds, as well as to battle. Copenhagen carried his master through the whole of the Battle of Waterloo and when he died in 1836 was buried at the Duke's home, Stratfield Saye, with the deserved epitaph: "God's humbler instrument though meaner clay, Should share the glory of that glorious day".

The Rifle Brigade had some remarkable pets which travelled with them. On the Feast of the Epiphany, 1900, Nell, the battalion terrier serving in South Africa during the Boer War, was safely delivered of twins who were named Shot and Shell. Also on the strength were a badger and two ibexes. A much-photographed dog of a previous generation was Teak Wood, the liver and white spaniel whose name, like the names of Henry's daughters, was a pun. But the most

14. Olive Wood, the colonel's daughter dressed fashionably in a sailor suit, poses for Papa

eccentric of all the Rifle Brigade pets (or any other regimental pets
for that matter) was surely "Doctor Dakins". This raven was only
too well known by the wives who kept hens in barracks as a thief of
eggs and baby chicks, and few can have missed him when he sailed
for America with his battalion in 1842. A great misfortune overtook
the poor Doctor on the voyage. During a high wind he was blown
overboard and the ship sailed on, leaving him "small as a bottle"
bobbing up and down on the rough sea. So impressed was the captain of the vessel by the men's distress that he actually ordered the
ship to turn about. When it got near enough Doctor Dakins was still
bobbing and was brought safely aboard by the sailors who jumped
into the water to rescue him. Unharmed by his ordeal, which was
surprising since he was already five years old, he reached America
in safety and died in 1844 two years later.

Fanny Duberley's favourite horse, the grey whose name she
never could bring herself to speak, was given a sea burial off Malta
"when the calm evening was dressed in gorgeous colours—and military calls were sounding those stirring notes he loved to hear"
Lord Cardigan's beautiful bay, Ronald, survived her other horse
Bob, by several years. These two horses were a familiar feature of the
Crimean War, as their owners rode together long before the famous
charge of the Light Brigade. Ronald died in honourable retirement
in 1875. Juana Smith's Vitty never left her mistress and lived to
enjoy a peacetime existence.

A sergeant's wife obtained permission to bring a bull-calf, to
whom she had become devoted, home by troopship from the
Crimea. Another veteran from this campaign was Tom, the tabby
who attained a degree of immortality by sitting for his portrait on his
return to England. Now, stuffed but still belligerent, he glares at
visitors to the Military Museum in Chelsea. A dog who survived the
horrors of Cawnpore died on the ship on the voyage home
apparently from cholera. The Polehamptons had a dog called Chloe
but no mention is made of her going into the Residency with them
The Reverend P. Harris, Henry Polehampton's colleague, did take
Bustle and the dog was a great anxiety to Mrs. Harris, who could
find barely enough food to feed themselves. The Harrises were much
attached to their dog, a present from a soldier they had been kind to

15. Teak's grave; Hazel Wood composed the epitaph, but the child in the picture is her sister Olive, accompanied by her fox terrier, Bee

but feared that it would be kinder to destroy it, rather than let it starve. Private Henry Metcalfe, 32nd Regiment, describes in his chronicle how near the dog came to being shot.

> I was sitting in the verandah of the house where we were stationed. A gentleman came out of the house and held a beautiful white terrier dog by the chain. He asked if one of our men would shoot the dog—this man (I mean the soldier) said he would, as he wanted to empty his piece, for the purpose of cleaning it. He would have done it had I not interposed and asked the gentleman if I could have the dog to keep.

Mr. Harris thought Metcalfe would not have enough to feed himself and the dog either, but fortunately, sentiment prevailed over reason. As Mrs. Harris says in her diary "We were afraid we should have to condemn him to death as the most merciful way of getting rid of him, when this delightful man, who is on guard in this house, offered to take charge of him till betters days should come". Metcalfe found Bussell (his spelling) a useful companion, as on the occasions when he was inclined to drowsiness on sentry duty "the dog was sure to notice and catch my trousers between his teeth and shake me to keep me awake". In 1860, Metcalfe met the Harrises in Aldershot, where he was stationed. They were accompanied by the dog "who immediately recognised me and commenced jumping at me and cutting all sorts of joyful antics".

The grave of a cat belonging to the Sergeants' Mess of the Royal Welch Fusiliers in Hong Kong in 1901 was recently discovered. It records that Bob had served with his regiment in Galway, the Curragh, Aldershot, Manchester, Malta and Egypt since joining the army in 1887.

A fitting tribute to all this whole company of pets who form part of army family life in peace and war, and in so many different places is surely expressed on a headstone in the garden of Cooldanah Cottage, Murree, in India. "Here lies Teak, for nine years the faithful friend of Miss Hazel Mary Wood 'though he was only a dog'. Died August 1884".

References to Chapter 9

On the Face of the Waters, F. A. Steel
Works by Kipling
Works by Saki

The Chronicle of Private Metcalfe, Metcalfe, Cassell, 1953
A Memoir, Letters and Diary of the Rev. Henry Polehampton, Richard
    Bentley, 1858

10. *Home*

IT WOULD BE interesting to know how the wives settled down so far from home in Tangiers as early as 1675. What did they make of the language, the accommodation, the shopping, the food, the climate, homesickness and the dozen other problems the army wife of all ranks learns to take in her stride? Did Mrs. Venables take mountains of luggage to Jamaica, and did she find it easy to set up house in surroundings so different from the Protector's England? Alas that we shall never know! We must wait a century to read an early and most comprehensive journal kept by an army wife. For this, we are indebted to Anna Walker, wife of Colonel George Townsend Walker, 14th Foot. Anna portrays herself, quite unconsciously, as the doting wife of a lazy, selfish man, who hated work and loved the bottle. Regimental soldiering did not agree with Walker as she always called him. He preferred the straitened circumstances of half pay to the tedium and heat of Jamaica. Fortunately, he was sent to Germany, France and Italy "to study tactics" and the couple enjoyed high society in all these countries, notably Hamburg and Berlin. This pleasant jaunting came to an end in 1779. Anna notes with disappointment "Walker must be in readiness to take charge of a hundred recruits in Hillsea Barracks, not very pleasant news to us, who hoped to be at liberty till the return of the regiment."

The Walkers bought and equipped a house in Queen Anne Street, London, for the inclusive price of £1352 2s. 8d., and it was no doubt due to Anna's careful accounting that they lived so comfortably. Their annual insurance for the house was 15 shillings, very moderate in comparison with the powder tax which cost £2 each for Anna and the manservant.

They ate very well, as the provision list for a coach journey from London to Manchester shows. "Currant jelly, trifle, woodcocks, salt fish and mackerel, pickled salmon, oysters, teal, lemons, two casks table beer, tops and bottoms, bread, butter, etc." When at home, Anna went in for bulk-buying and ordered meat 40 pounds at a time. Port wine cost £1 13s. 3d. per dozen bottles and was doubtless responsible for the frequent entries to the effect that "Walker was very unwell", had "one of his headaches", or was again unwell "in consequence of eating lobsters last night".

"Dressing for poor Caesar's skin" at 12s. 6d. was more expensive than cough mixture for the family at half a guinea. What was the present bought for 18s. and how many hair pencils (whatever they were) were purchased for the shillings expended? Walker's powder puff, one pound of powder pomatum, cost 2s. 6d. and nine sacks of coal, £1 16s. 8½d. Bonnet and ribbons at 5s. 8d. seems expensive against "pair little girl's shoes 1s., own shoes 4s. 6d.". She paid 8d. to have an earring mended and 9d. for "cordial balls for the horse", 1s. 10d. for window cleaning and 7½d. for pens and wax. The dog got lost one day and the "crier and reward" made an incidental expense of 8s. 6d., and she paid 10s. 6d to have a tooth out. Walker's portrait cost £10 and "miniature of self and Bab", £8 8s. od. Confinement expenses are carefully noted. The nurse received £10 for the month, her doctor £4 8s 6d. for the delivery and £10 as a present "between friends". Calico, flannel, cot drapings and powder puff "for the little baby" totted up to £2 11s. 4d. These and other items amounted to an annual expenditure of £788 16s. 4½d. She does not specify what Walker paid for two horses at Tattersalls, and the entry recording their purchase is followed by the brief, surprising note "Harriet had her stays tried".

Nor does she, unfortunately, describe the finery she wore when they dined with the Prince Regent, or repeat what, if anything, Prinny said to her. There is no mention of Walker being unwell, or having even the suspicion of a headache as they drove home through rackety Regency London at seven o'clock in the morning. Dining out was not always so enjoyable. On one occasion, she set out feeling so ill, she did not know how she was to get through the evening. She had to exercise the strongest self-control to support the attentions of a well-meaning fellow guest, who insisted on talking to her to try and keep her spirits up.

Anna is an outstanding example of the best kind of army wife; cheerful, uncomplaining, and able to enjoy herself wherever she is. There is no criticism of "my Walker's" selfishness, not even on the

occasion when he returned from some jaunt abroad to find her in
bed having been delivered of a daughter a few hours before, and he
immediately left the house to celebrate the happy event and his own
return. Only once does she register being in really low spirits, which
is not surprising since she was in agony with a bad breast abscess.
Duty did eventually catch up with Walker and he was dispatched
(unwillingly no doubt) to the Peninsula. There he was actually
exposed to sufficient danger to get wounded and Anna hurried out to
visit the hero. Theirs was evidently a happy marriage, no matter
what she had to put up with over Walker's hangovers and general
behaviour. She accepted him for what he was, she loved him and
they suited each other. Surviving him by several years, she died in
late middle age after an enjoyable evening spent at a party.

Anna was more fortunate than Charlotte Owen (see p. 119) in that
she could buy her silks and ribbons, her bonnets and boots, over the
counter. Charlotte's order went over the sea and back again in
journeys that took months. Her directions as to what she wanted
were precise. "Two pairs stays, four pairs long white gloves, six pairs
short white, six pairs short coloured. One and a half yards of green
plaid ribbon, one and a half yards of lemon, blue and pink, twenty-
four yards of black ribbon the length of the narrow sarcenet".

Clothes were a matter of importance to the army wife. For
officers' wives in the very rich regiments, there was no problem.
They could be, and were, as beautifully dressed at Royal Ascot,
London theatres and Buckingham Palace garden parties as any other
wife in what would have been called the front ranks of society. But
the average army wife needed quite a large number of clothes on a
not very large income. To turn herself out as most of them did
required considerable thought, budgeting and ingenuity.

Clothes fell into clearly-defined categories. The coat and skirt
(no-one said "two-piece", and "costume" was something between a
music-hall joke and a dirty word) that you wore for point-to-points
was not smart enough to wear at the Grand National, though both
could be made by the same tailor, and were never bought off-the-
peg. The riding habit was an essential part of the wardrobe. If you
were rich, you went to Busvine, and if not so rich, to Collard. Mr.

Collard fitted you himself in the 1920s and 30s in the small, dark fitting room he visited once a week in Reading or, if you could make the journey, in Swindon, where he had his business. Many women still rode side-saddle up to the Second World War and a habit for hunting cost well under £20, while a thinner one for hacking cost considerably less. Ladies bought their hats, top or bowler, from Mrs. White, Jermyn Street. The rich had their boots made by Maxwell, but there were many excellent bootmakers in the country towns. Saddles came from Champion and Wilton, Wippy or Owen, made to a horse's individual measurements or on a "general fitting tree".

There was a great deal of dining-out and entertaining at home, which meant evening dresses, at least six of them at a time. The wedding dress was the best evening dress for the year. Many army brides had been presented as débutantes and it was considered desirable that they should make their curtsey again on marriage. Clothes for this were special. A really grand evening dress (12 guineas would have been considered a fair price for this before the last war), feathers and a wisp of white tulle to be attached to the back of the head (three guineas), and a bouquet or feather fan. The whole extraordinary outfit was completed by a train attached to the shoulders and trailing for a regulation number of inches on the ground behind. Following the death of a sovereign, officers wore black ties and armbands and their wives wore black in public for a minimum of three months.

Fanny Duberley was very particular about her clothes and, like many an army wife since, dressed well by making many of them herself. She favoured high-necked dresses for day, and stripes and satins of the evenings, when she entertained in her leafy bower. She wrote continually to her sister, Selina, for materials. Fanny was a show-off, and was upset and annoyed when a Zouave riding habit in which she hoped to cut a dash was not finished in time for her to wear on the particular occasion for which she ordered it. She writes unkindly about an officer's wife whose clothes were awful, her complexion battered and her appearance unkempt.

Another adverse comment on an officer's wife and what she wore is made by Colonel Edward Hodge, 4th Light Dragoons, who writes in his diary on a date in 1855 "that horrid Mrs. Forrest is still here (in the Crimea). She has no maid, but a great he-dragon to do all she wants". The he-dragon was observed on October 13th "picking the fleas out of Mrs. F's drawers, after which he hung them out to dry".

Mountains of luggage rolled and rattled over Europe with the army and its families. Hump-backed trunks, bonnet boxes, silver chests and chests of drawers, all survived campaigning to become treasured heirlooms. One of the dancers at the Duchess of Richmond's ball on the eve of the Battle of Waterloo wore a charming dress of sprigged cotton, which returned to Jersey with her after the war was over. Carefully preserved as a family treasure, it was left in the house in the hurried evacuation of 1940, found by the German soldiers billeted there and used as cleaning material for their rifles. It must have been a source of envy and annoyance to Fanny and other wives, shabby after so much campaigning, when visitors appeared in the Crimea to watch the battles from safe vantage points, their exquisite crinolines, the newest fashion, spread round them as they picnicked off delicacies supplied by the shipping company who ran the tours.

Of all the girls whose tiny waists were made tinier by the spread of these enormous skirts, none ever looked more ravishing than Frances, the nineteen-year-old bride of Major Henry Wood, who, a decade later, posed for her husband's photographs in her drawing-room, seated among ruined temples or reclining in a boat in Kashmir.

Fancy dress was very popular. Britannias, butterflies, pierrettes, and Pompadours, swayed and twirled on the arms of Henry VIII, Friar Tuck, Beau Brocade or Mephistopheles, in any part of the world the army happened to be. It would never have occurred to ninety per cent of the sovereign's forces that their social pleasures, which they took where and when they wanted with such splendid arrogance, might ever have appeared outlandish or undignified to people of other cultures. Flora Annie Steel, an acute observer of the British, as well as the Indian scene, shows that the social activities of the army could make a very bad impression indeed. In her novel *On The Face Of The Waters*, there is a telling little scene, obviously

16. In the 1880s a lady wearing her dressing gown, hair loose and down her back, and pregnant at that, would simply not have had her photograph taken—except by her husband, Henry Wood!

drawn from life. An Englishman and a woman friend stroll through
an Indian fair, stumbling on a side-show "which" says the writer
made them "stand transfixed". Two white-masked figures waltzed
tipsily, clasped waist to waist. Both were men, but one wore a flaxen
wig and a muslin dress, whose crinoline skirt could not hide the
prancing brown legs. The yellow head rested on the shoulders of the
tarnished epaulette of its partner, who wore an old staff uniform
cocked hat and feather complete, and flourished a brandy bottle.

It was at once the army's social strength and its greatest weakness
that it made few concessions to scene or circumstance. From Mrs
General to Mrs. Corporal, they took Camberley/Catterick
Aldershot/Colchester or wherever and set it up in miniature in
Gib/Shanghai/Lucknow/Rangoon/Singapore and a dozen other
places. Houses or quarters followed the same pattern with regard to
décor and furnishing. It was important to look as chintzy and
country-house as possible.

Food too. Wherever you were in the world, you could be sure of
what you would get in greater or lesser degree of excellence at an
army dinner party: clear soup with small squares of savoury baked
custard added before serving; fish to follow, usually rolled fillets of
plaice with shrimp sauce, though from a colonel's wife upwards, it
could be Dover sole. The cutlets, egged and breadcrumbed, wore
paper frills on their tails and were arranged round a mound of
mashed potato. The accompanying vegetables varied according to
season. A pudding, lemon soufflé probably, would be followed by a
savoury, usually "angels on horseback" (prunes wrapped in bacon
rashers and balanced on rounds of fried bread), or "devil's ditto"
(chicken liver served the same way with chutney added). After this
the soldier servant, who had handed round all the food assisted by
parlourmaid, if the household could run to one, cleared the table and
produced dessert plates, each with its pearl-handled silver knife and
fork to cut the fruit, and finger bowls half filled with water. The
fruit would also vary according to income, as did the sweets
and chocolates in little bowls that were part of the table
decoration.

The wife was responsible for all the food and her husband saw to the wine and the port. It was also her unhappy lot to turn a fairly raw private soldier into an imitation butler and see that his white jacket was crisp and clean. A good soldier servant was invaluable, and even the less good were usually willing and amiable. But they had not joined the army to wait at table and the wife who had a real treasure who would work as well for her as he did for the master was lucky indeed. The dessert service was a necessary part of household equipment, as were the plates whose curved line followed that of the meat plates, alongside which they were laid, and which were used for salad. Famous in army households was a curious dish called "beef olives", though according to Mrs. Beeton, no olive was ever actually involved. It is possible, if not wholly probable, that strips of rump steak wrapped round forcemeat and cooked in good rich gravy made an enjoyable dish. At some forgotten date, however, it became the standby of the inexperienced wife who had to rely on her cook-general, herself, or the soldier servant to do whatever they could with ration meat. The result was horrible little packages tied round with string (which was sometimes left on by mistake) tasting of packet stuffing, the gravy made with meat cubes.

Entertaining and all social recreations were carried out within a well-defined framework, the prop of which was "Calling", or "Writing One's Name In The Book".

Both of these were of paramount importance. Omit either and you could be an outcast. The bachelors called and left cards on the married households of their own regiments if they did not already know them, on such households of other regiments that they wished to get to know, and on any married staff officer and his wife. Married women did the same with couples of superior rank to their husbands' and there was, of course, "The Book".

This was of such sacred importance that it usually occupied a special place of its own; the porch of Flagstaff House, home of the Divisional Commander, or a small room at the gate of a Governor's residence. Everybody had to, repeat had to, write their name in one or both of these books immediately on arrival in a station. This was an obligation as binding as the marriage vow.

One wife remembers being whisked round a large Indian station

204 ON THE STRENGTH

to register with Government House, Flagstaff House and the COs (cards only) of the existing regiments before her husband had even been allotted a quarter for them to live in. A married woman left three calling cards. One from herself to the wife, as it would not have been etiquette for her to call on a gentleman, and two from her husband, as it was quite proper for him to call on both. To take leave of a Governor or Commander-in-Chief, cards were left with the letters "p.p.c.": "*pour prendre congé*" written at the bottom, and the lower right hand corner turned up.

All officers and all wives had a supply of visiting cards, which had always to be engraved. A printed card put you beyond the pale. Married majors and upwards were asked to dinner in high places, provided they had fulfilled all the conditions. Captains and their wives might make it as far as a garden party, and the rest neither expected nor received invitations.

That the army had a riproaring good time was known, with envy, by everybody in all walks of life. A sergeants' dance in a regimental gym or drill hall was a lavish affair, very different from the hop in the village hall. Men in scarlet, and wives and sweethearts dressed to kill, swinging through the valeta, military two-step, or the palais glide: it was a splendid happening with its own uninhibited beauty. Officers and their wives attended these dances by invitation, but were rarely as expert in performance as Mrs. Sergeant and her husband.

Major John Patterson has left an amusing description of a military ball in Ireland in the late 1830s.

In the country town where we were quartered, we were called on and generously entertained by all the respectable people of the neighbourhood, in return for which it was agreed to treat them with a ball and supper. The entertainment was altogether so unequalled by anything of the kind that ever took place in these parts before or since, that it is but an act of justice to posterity to put the affair on record, for the improvement and example, as well as for the information, of the said posterity.

There were problems over the invitations, as "the aristocratic tribe" might not mix well with those whose lineage was shorter, but who had, nevertheless, been very kind to the military. "Those minor points of etiquette being at last arranged to the satisfaction of all concerned, the long looked for day arrived, big with the fate of subalterns and spinsters". One can imagine the flutter. The dashing English regiment; the looks and sighs and longings; the hopes of mamma and probably of papa too, who might well be relieved at having a daughter or two off his aristocratic, but impoverished hands. There was a master of ceremonies stationed at the gateway "to prevent confusion", i.e. sort out gate-crashers from invitation holders and get rid of the former. Inside, the barrack building, all passages and stairways were "lined with cloth and baize and illumined with the King's own tapers" (in other words, drawn from stores). When "the lively throng ascended to the ballroom", the doors were thrown open and "a gorgeous display burst upon the enraptured vision", a sight beyond the powers of language. The enraptured guests looked across the floor chalked with emblematic devices to where on the far wall was "a grand transparent painting of some warlike subject, surmounted by a star of bayonets". The band "blew away" and among the dancers, the "animated looks and laughing eyes of the Irish beauties bounding to the enlivening music", expressed "the joy that was passing in their hearts". Encouraging this, for mammas "anxious, if possible, to establish the embryo of a matrimonial spec". The few poor wallflowers referred to strike a sad little note amid the gaiety.

The surprise of the evening was an impromptu cabaret turn, given by one of the regimental ladies "of amazonian build, a regular first rate in build and mettle. On the Highland Fling being called for, she pounded the floor in capital style" till the very floor seemed in danger. Her partner being a subaltern from Fifeshire, and she herself a Scot "she clapped her hands as a condor would his wings for the music to play faster, faster still, jumped high and tossed her slippers into the air, shouting 'Hoo, Scotland forever, hurra'" to thundering applause. After this, everyone repaired to supper, where "the delicate viands were stormed" and game, pastries, sweetmeats, jellies and kickshaws in abundance all "vanished with lightning speed".

Theatricals were an accepted part of army life and some stations had their own theatres. Many a romance began behind the footlights, though it must be admitted that there was often a certain sameness about the performances. The producer was frequently a senior officer, who was in a position to choose his players and take the leading male role himself. A hardy annual was the Staff College pantomime, full of in-jokes which were mainly incomprehensible to civilians.

But it wasn't all social gas and gaiters. Life could be hard for the family with little more than their pay as income, particularly when the time came to educate the children. Up to the Second World War, it would have been unthinkable on the part of officer parents to allow their children to be educated abroad. It sometimes happened that the mother returned with them to Britain, running a tiny rented home more economically than paying relatives or guardians, while the husband gave up his horse and most other amusements, and lived a life of spartan loneliness in order that his son might be educated at his own old school.

Wives had to make light of the difficulties of bringing up a family while constantly moving from posting to posting. Forty homes in half as many years, the shortest time in any of them being two weeks this was the married life of Mrs. Molly Bruxner-Randall, and must surely be a record for any army wife. In the intervals of packing and unpacking, letting down curtains or taking them up, spreading furniture over rooms too large or cramming it into those too small she bore and brought up her children with little time or inclination to reflect that this was not everyone's way of living.

Mrs. Bruxner-Randall had had, however, a far more brutal than usual initiation into what the life of an army wife might entail. It occurred on a summer day in 1921 when her parents were giving a party at their home in Ireland, shortly before Molly's marriage to Captain Bruxner-Randall of The Royal Welch Fusiliers. Here is her story told in her own words, fifty years later:

"In the summer of 1921, a company of the 17th Lancers was stationed in Gort some four miles away from my home in County Galway. Most Sundays, some of them would come out to Ballyturi to have tea with us and play tennis. On May 21st, Captain Cornwall and Lieutenant McCreery, together with Captain Blake of the Roy-

Irish Constabulary, drove over by car to see us. They brought with them Blake's wife and Mrs. Gregory, the daughter-in-law of Lady Gregory, the Irish writer.

At about 7 o'clock, they decided to leave, only to discover that they had a puncture. McCreery and Cornwallis, however, quickly changed the wheel and then they all set off down the drive to the main road some threequarters of a mile away.

My sister and I went upstairs to start changing for dinner. We had only been in our rooms a few minutes when Paddy, the groom, rushed into the hall and shouted up to us that he had heard the sound of shots coming from the direction of the end of the drive.

My father and the gamekeeper joined us as we hurried down through the woods, taking the short-cut to the gate. This brought us out on to the drive a few hundred yards from the road. As we crossed the bridge which took the drive over a small stream, we could just see the car. We could now guess what happened.

Somebody had closed one of the gates and on arriving at them, Captain Blake had stopped the car for Cornwallis to get out and open it. As he, Captain Cornwallis, was pulling it (the gate) inwards, a shot came from bushes on the right, with a shout of 'Hands up'. Two other shots followed from the same point, breaking the windscreen. Lieutenant McCreery and Mrs. Blake scrambled out and took cover on the left of the car, Captain Blake and Mrs. Gregory following. Intense fire was then opened by about ten men (some masked with white rags and others with blackened faces) who gradually worked round to the front and left of the car. Mrs. Gregory then got round to the back of the car, but Mrs. Blake refused to leave her husband. After three or four minutes, the firing ceased with a heavy volley at close range. Captain and Mrs. Blake and Lieutenant McCreery were all dead. While their bodies were searched, Mrs. Gregory was allowed to go. Captain Cornwallis had taken cover outside the wall to the right of the gate and was killed by a shot in the back.

Suddenly, two men stepped from the bushes and held us up at gunpoint. We were told not to move. While they were deciding among themselves what to do with us, I decided to try and slip away. By moving a few yards every time the guards were not looking, I managed to get closer to the trees on the side of the drive and when I thought I was within running distance of cover I took to my heels. I ran through the woods as fast as I could, trying to think what I should do. As I turned into the stable yard, Paddy, who had also managed to get away, caught up with me.

I sent him off to get the pony and together we put it into the trap and set off across the fields to Gort to get help. This way round would be about eight miles instead of four, but at any rate it was unlikely to be barred by the extremists as the main road obviously was.

We drove straight to the barracks in Gort to find the sergeant in charge and explain what had happened. The horror of it all suddenly came home to Paddy and he was violently sick. With about twenty soldiers and police, we went back by the main road to Ballyturin.

When we got to the gates we found that the lodge-keeper and his son and daughter had been forcibly kept in the lodge by the extremists for five hours and had been able to see the ambush without being able to do anything about it.

As the soldiers and police started to search the grounds, a shot rang out. We threw ourselves to the ground, but Sergeant Carney, RIC, fell dead just behind me. What happened afterwards remained a merciful blank."

Thus it came about that when Miss Molly Bagott married Captain Bruxner-Randall, they were given two silver salvers among their wedding presents instead of the regulation one. The second one was unique, recording the gratitude of the officers of the 17th Lancers for Miss Bagott's bravery on that summer day in Ireland. Her silver salvers became part of the paraphernalia which accompanied her on her family's moves through forty homes in twenty years—a career which must surely have demanded all the presence of mind which she once so ably demonstrated.

The wife who did not fit into the pattern was something of a white blackbird. It is not for nothing that one has always heard of the "typical army wife". It could be said, at any rate on the face of it, that she was rather a superficial creature, rather gay or rather dull according to her circumstances, capable but not over-intelligent, amusing but not intellectually witty, and not obviously a seeker after the deeper levels of life and the spirit.

But while it is true to say that most army folk would have found it embarrassing, if not indecent, to so much as mention any spiritual doubts or longings, it is equally true that in a peculiar, rather Mithraic way, most of them were sincerely religious. The reverence for regimental colours; the adopting and dedication of regimental chapels in church and cathedral, where the faded colours hanging overhead speak emotively of past glories, and the congregations kneel on hassocks devotedly embroidered by the ladies of the regiment. The assertion of many a war memorial that the commemorated dead had demonstrated the ultimate love by laying down their lives for their friends, was not really true to eyes which read the names with hindsight, knowing that their fathers and grandfathers went to war because it was their job or because they were conscripted. Nevertheless, it was an assertion made in good faith and a consolation to thousands who mourned. The Last Post sounding over a grave, the unconsciously mystical importance attached to regimental animal mascots, the British Legion banners carried proudly in the Festival of Remembrance, the eating of the leek and drinking the toast to Dewi Sant from a communal cup—the whole extraordinary blend of Christianity and paganism made up the army's own brand of piety. The General who found the singing of the Creed irreverent would have had no similar difficulty over Kipling's "Soldier's Prayer", in which the Roman Legionary invokes "Mithras, god of the morning". Few men, and even fewer women, not brought up, or at least married into the army, can even begin to fathom the depths of this archaic heritage; part of the air the army wife breathed, part of daily living, something she never took much account of till retirement came and it was over.

Except, and this is where the army wife is luckier than most, it never really ended. "Old soldiers never die, they only fade away" is also true of their wives. No organisation of any kind anywhere can have fulfilled the needs, physical and emotional, of its members as has the army. Need and fulfilment evolved side by side over centuries, the result of lessons learned (often slowly) from victory and

14

defeat, indifference and concern. The blunt, unintellectual, pig-headed, bloody-minded British soldier, from Field Marshal to private, lived, fought, married, begat children and retired within an extra-ordinary mystique as powerful and binding as the mediaeval church. Its famous spit and polish corresponded to ecclesiastical ritual, a ritual carried out over everything from the shine painfully acquired after repeated cursing by the company sergeant-major on the boots of the newest recruit, the title of "goat major" borne by the man who cared for a white billy with gilded horns and silver trappings, the gleam of candlelight on regimental silver reflected in a polished table, band instruments blazing in the sun, to the splendour of a Sovereign's escort, and, most beautiful and sacred of all, the Trooping of the Colour.

No wonder Kim, peering through the tent flap of the officers' mess tent of the Mavericks on the march, got a bit confused. "It was as he suspected. The sahibs prayed to their God; for in the centre of the mess table—its sole ornament when they were on the line of march—stood a bull, a red gold bull with lowered head, ramping on a field of Irish green. To him the sahibs held out their glasses and cried aloud confusedly".

All this mystique and ceremonial belonged to the soldier; but his wife, since she bore the sons who so often followed their fathers into the army, was, though unacknowledged, as much a part of it as he was. That there were many families where it would be unthinkable that the boys became anything but soldiers can be proved by annual copies of that official Bible, the Army List.

Retirement from the army was in no way comparable with retire-ment from anything else. No gold watch, or any other kind of presentation: the "gongs" gleaming on bright ribbons on the lapel of the civvy suit at old comrades' parades had been earned in the days of youth and valour, and in many countries of the world. The faces in the framed photographs of X Company or the Nth Battalion were as familiar to the wives who dusted them as to their husbands whose messmates they had been. The soldier and his wife were lucky in retirement in that they were seldom lonely.

Many retired within reach of the regimental depot, or the garrisons where they had courted their wives. For the officers, places like Camberley and Cheltenham were agreeable and not too expensive. It was now that the wife came into her own, no longer a sort of adjunct to the mess. The situation was probably easier in most cases for the wives than for the ladies, as the latter often had to lower certain social standards. Rent and the soldier servant were no longer perks and civilian living was a good deal more expensive. But one kept in touch. Friends from the good old days turned up, there was the regimental dinner at a London club or hotel held in June in London, with a get-together of wives and a cocktail party next day.

Widowed wives of senior officers held an honoured position in the affection and regard of their husbands' regiments. Mrs. Webber Harris's home in London was a little kingdom in which she kept court into old age, while one of the most remarkable army widows was "Aunt Louise" of The King's Shropshire Light Infantry. She married Lieutenant E. B. Luard in 1905, while he was a captain and went with him to India and then to Ireland. From there the regiment went to France after the outbreak of war. Louise plunged immediately into war work which she interrupted only to get herself across to France at short notice to spend her husband's leaves with him in Paris. She founded the KSLI prisoner of war fund, working tirelessly as its honorary secretary and treasurer. Colonel Luard was killed in 1916 and from then on, in spite of increasing public commitments which included two terms as Mayor of Hereford (the only woman to have held that office), her chief concern was the welfare of the men, women and children of her husband's regiment. It was said she knew them all by name and to one and all she was Aunt Louise.

In recognition of her work for the prisoners of war she was awarded the OBE in 1920 and in the same year she received another honour which, though unofficial, she valued even more. At a parade of the 2nd Battalion, stationed once more at the Curragh, she was presented with the regimental badge in diamonds, a token of the gratitude of all ranks. She inaugurated a regimental beneficent fund with a handsome donation from herself in memory of her husband, and her close ties with The King's Shropshire Light Infantry ceased only with her death in 1945. Few if any other regiments can boast a "regimental aunt" who nearly 30 years after her death is remembered with so much admiration, affection and respect.

Mrs. Evans, of Crimean fame, was photographed in old age, wearing her husband's medals (by permission of the colonel of the regiment) and holding the hand of one of a group of the Chelsea pensioners she visited from her home in Richmond. When she died, she was buried with full military honours, the coffin covered with a Union Jack and the regimental pall inscribed with its battle honours. Mrs. Butler, another Crimean heroine, had men of the 1st Dorset Regiment to bear her to her grave and her name was inscribed in her husband's regimental book of remembrance.

Few women make their way into official regimental histories. One who did so, while still in her twenties, was the wife of Lieutenant Colonel Edmund Wodehouse, commanding the 2nd Battalion, The Royal Welch Fusiliers, in September 1939. The battalion was stationed in Lucknow and in May 1940, was ordered home at five days' notice. "In this predicament so suddenly forced upon them," says the history, "Mrs. Wodehouse was a tower of strength, comforting the wives and children and herself taking over arrangements for keeping in touch with husbands and fathers".

From time to time, and long before retiring age, an officer could go on half pay, which could last for up to two or three years, five in the case of ill-health. The rates descended from £1300 p.a. for a Field Marshal to 3s. per day for a second lieutenant. This situation was not easy for the wife, as the family was not entitled to quarters or allowances. In 1827, an offer was made to officers on half pay "to become settlers in New South Wales and Van Diemen's Land— officers of all ranks on half pay are eligible, they are not required to sell their half pay or make any deposit. The officer who will avail himself of this offer will be required to provide for his own passage and that of his family". A cabin passage to New South Wales cost £94 10s., steerage £40, and to Van Diemen's Land, it was £10 and £5 cheaper respectively. A reduction of £10 for cabin passengers and £5 for those going steerage was made if man and wife shared the same bunk. Children from nine to 13 years travelled at two-thirds the adult fee, from five to eight years, at half, from two to four, at a quarter, and those over 14 as adults. Everything was supplied for the voyage except bedding, which the passengers supplied themselves. Heavy goods were carried in the hold at £4 per ton and "measurement goods" (articles of furniture) at £5 for the same weight.

Rather curiously, the army, which neglected its wives for so long while their husbands were alive, did not entirely neglect its widows, even from the earliest days, although their situation was never an enviable one. In 1646, a committee of the House of Commons, appointed for officers and soldiers' widows, sitting in the Inner Chamber of the Court of Wards, ordered that the sum of 40 pounds a week paid to the Earl of Mulgrave should, since the Earl was now deceased, be paid to the use of widows "in such manner as the said order is exprest". By the beginning of the eighteenth century, there were two established ways of raising money for pensions. Officers paid a tax into the Widows' Fund, and in all regiments, except those fighting in Flanders, a "Widows' Man" was appointed. This fictitious character drew a statutory rate of pay, which went into the fund for officers' widows. In Marlborough's army, the widows were supported by voluntary subscriptions from the officers, but the fund was unable to meet the demand. In 1709, the Duke had to ask for "Widows' Men" to be commissioned to a proportion of his troops.

Occasionally, children were given commissions in the regiments their dead fathers had commanded and drew pay which went towards the widow's support, but this practice was ended by Royal Regulations in 1711. Orphaned boys were taken on the strength as trumpeters and the most famous of these was John Edwards. The bugle he blew on the field of Waterloo at the age of 15 now hangs in the Museum of the Household Cavalry at Windsor. The first widow to be mentioned is a Mrs. Wedderburn, whose husband, a major in Brigadier Sutton's Regiment, was killed at Dornay. In a letter dated, July 9th, 1710, the Duke of Marlborough requests a Colonel Newton to pay her £100 from a fund at his disposal. In 1766, a letter went from the War Office to commanding officers of all regiments, with proposals "for executing a scheme for maintaining and educating the infants and orphans of soldiers".

The Duke of Wellington, "Commander-in-Chief of the British

Army at Paris" received a letter in July 1815 from a committee
formed of London bankers, traders, merchants and others. They
informed him that, in their opinion, the best means of showing
their sense of obligation to those who had conquered at Waterloo
was to transmit to His Grace the subscription list opened for the
relief of the families of the brave men killed in that battle. At this
date, widows' pensions were fixed at amounts ranging from £120 p.a.
for the widow of a general, to the lowest of all, £30, for the widow
of a veterinary officer. A precedence of relatives was also laid down,
from a man's widow to a second cousin. Previously, a widow had
been entitled to a full year's pay, according to her husband's
commissioned rank, and for each child, posthumous children
included, a third of that amount. It was incumbent on the paymaster
of the corps "to which the deceased did belong" to defray the
passage and victualling of such women and children as were abroad
at the time of the soldier's death home to Great Britain or Ireland.
While the right to a pension belonged generally to widows and
orphans and the cases of their being paid to second cousins must
have been relatively few, to a bereaved mother deprived of financial
help from a soldier son, the modest sum allotted could make a world
of difference between respectable poverty and the shaming
experience of "going on the parish".

One such mother was Mrs. McCabe. Her son had entered the
army as a private and risen to the commissioned rank of major
when he was killed at Lucknow. Mrs. McCabe had good cause to be
proud of her boy, whose bravery made a deep impression on Sir
Harry Smith at the Battle of Sobraon, on General Lord Gough, on
Lady Inglis, who records in her diary that "poor McCabe was
carried past our door, shot through the lungs", and on Sergeant
Metcalfe at whose side he fell. Metcalfe records that "the Commander in Chief recommended that this officer's mother might
receive a pension, as this, her son, was the sole means of her support,
so that being a good officer, he was also a good and dutiful son".
Metcalfe, who always noted the cheerful things of life whenever
possible, adds with evident satisfaction "his mother got the
annuity and, if alive, is drawing it now and may she continue to
do so".

Less fortunate was Mrs. Molloy, whose husband, Dr. William Talbot Malloy, died on service with the Northampton Militia at Gibraltar in 1855. The family was brought back to Dublin, Mrs. Molloy ill with a malady contracted in Gibraltar, probably the dysentery from which her husband died. This is a weakening complaint, in the course of which the patient passes blood through the stools. Mrs. Molloy had no means of support for herself and her four children other than help given by relatives and kindly friends. A claim was launched on her behalf, but unsuccessfully, since there was no provision made to provide pensions for the widows of militiamen. The poor woman struggled along for a year and then died, leaving her family, the eldest ten years old, to be a continued charge on others or go on the parish.

It was often difficult for a widow to establish her right to a pension. Mrs. Butler, who had endured the whole of the Crimean campaign, never succeeded, partly because of the age-old army reluctance to admit that any man who subsequently died of ill health had been adversely affected by wounds or war, and partly because she had 2s. outdoor relief and took in sewing. After she had given written evidence on behalf of 500 Crimean widows who had also been unsuccessful, she was given a pension of 5s. per week, and a further weekly 2s. on reaching the age of seventy. With the introduction of the Old Age Pension and her successful application for it, the secretary of the Patriotic Fund informed her that her army widow's pension would cease forthwith. She was 80 years old and in poor physical health. After an officer of the 95th Regiment, in which her husband had done all his service, had taken up her case, 3s. 6d. per week was restored to her.

Considering the rough, tough life they had to lead, it is amazing that so many army wives have lived into very ripe old age. In the graveyard of Tal y llyn, Merionethshire, a tombstone informs the passer-by that a certain Jenny Jones was born in 1789 and died in April 1884. What distinguishes her from the neighbours who sleep round her, apart from her great age, is the fact that "she was with her husband of the 23rd Royal Welch Fusiliers at the Battle of Waterloo and was on the field three days". She must surely have delighted friends, relatives and the young with splendid stories —or bored them to distraction by determined repetition!

Another Mrs. Jones, Ann, wife of a sergeant in the Montgomery Militia, always found ready listeners in her tribe of grandchildren for the stories she used to tell of the days when as "a slip of a girl", she marched from North to South Wales as one of 37 regimental washerwomen. On a fine day in 1855, the militia set out from Welshpool for Pembroke Dock, where they were to replace the regiment ordered from that garrison to the Crimea. For Ann Jones, it was a great day. Wives on the strength and entitled to go accompanied the men, marching in front and headed by Mrs. Jenny Gilmour and the pet nanny goat she led. Evidently, Mrs. Gilmour was not on the strength, nor the nanny either, as they had to return from Shrewsbury, where the regiment entrained for Newport in Monmouthshire. The crowds, "hundreds and hundreds of people" who had lined the streets and many of whom marched a distance alongside the soldiery, turned back at last. Men and women of the militia settled down to slog the rest of the 20 miles to Shrewsbury. Mrs. Jones was lucky and got a lift on a waggon. From Newport, they marched to Haverfordwest, where they spent the night, proceeding next day to Pembroke Dock and their quarters in the barracks.

Ann enjoyed herself enormously. "Some of us who had not seen so much before thought we must be getting to the end of the world." The older sergeants' wives "who had travelled about nearly all over the world" were kind to the younger ones and "used to help us". There was plenty of work for the women to do. Each washerwoman had to look after 27 men and received pay at the rate of $3\frac{1}{2}$d. per man. "For that, we had to wash two shirts, a towel, haversacks, a hold-all and other things—the Welshpool Town Hall was nothing to the size of that wash house. All the washing was done by hand, there were no machines, not even rubbing boards." They all took great pride in their work. "I can tell you, those men were kept clean" Mrs. Jones assured her grandchildren. There was plenty to eat and the cook was "a black man, a right nice fellow". They all had a surprise one morning when "about one o'clock, an alarm was given and everyone was called up. We all got outside pretty quick, I can tell you, but it proved to be nothing, only a false alarm." Mrs. Jones was sorry when the orders came to return to Welshpool. Laundry money was good. "I went from home with a sovereign in my pocket, and I came back with seven, not to mention silver." When they got out of the train at Shrewsbury on the return journey, there was Mrs. Jenny Gilmour and the nanny goat to lead them back to Welshpool and the grand welcome the town gave them. Jenny Gilmour, Mary Pryce, another sergeant's wife, and Ann Jones remained friends all their lives. Ann outlived both, and her husband, raising seven children. Her sons were good footballers, and, at the age of 87, she still took pride and interest in the local team, of which her grandson was goalkeeper. At 83 she declined a free trip in an aeroplane, but continued to enjoy good health for several more years, the secret of this being "hard work, plenty of good food taken with a glass of beer, and sleeping like a top". She died full of years and wisdom in 1926, and her claim to have been the last of the army washerwomen might very well be true.

Years, wisdom and happy memories. These were the true old-age pension of the army wife. The pity of it is that comparatively few ever recorded for posterity. This is understandable, though, since for her, above all people, life was for living, and she was always busy getting on with the job. There is certainly a well of untapped material tucked away in the proverbial attic, old boxes and country archives, which has never seen the light of day and hardly ever been read for anything up to a hundred years. But let the aspiring researcher beware. The fine spidery handwriting has faded to eye-straining paleness. The letters which give such graphic accounts of comedy as well as tragedy are written on thin paper, brittle now, and overwritten vertically to economise on space and weight. The handwriting is nearly always beautiful, resulting from the careful pothooks and copying of early learning, but though there is no slipshod scribbling, there are word abbreviations which make for slight confusion. Great-grandmother, her sisters and daughters all wrote home faithfully and their letters, if still extant, tell of goings-on which would have defeated most women of any age and make one's hair stand on end today. Why on earth did they not record it all properly with dates and all that sort of thing? And the Victorian custom of giving a baby the name or names of its little dead predecessor can cause endless confusion. How could they write about the amazing things that happened as if they were so ordinary? Because they were ordinary, that's why. Nothing to it. We were army wives. This was our life.

References to Chapter 10

Kim, R. Kipling, Macmillan, 1908
On the Face of the Waters, F. A. Steel
The Siege of Lucknow, Lady Inglis, Osgood & McIlvaine, 1892
Scenes and Impressions of Military Life, Major J. Patterson, Saunders &
    Ottley, 1840

The Chronicle of Private Metcalfe, Metcalfe, Cassell, 1953
*Little Hodge: extracts from the diaries and letters of Col. Edward Cooper
    Hodge, written during the Crimean War, 1854–56*, ed. The Marquess of
    Anglesey, Leo Cooper, 1971

Index

Printed in Great Britain by
Ebenezer Baylis & Son Ltd.
The Trinity Press, Worcester, and London